Refresher Course in GREGG SHORTHAND SIMPLIFIED

Madeline S. Strony

M. Claudia Garvey

Howard L. Newhouse

Shorthand Written by CHARLES RADER

GREGG PUBLISHING DIVISION
McGraw-Hill Book Company, Inc.

New York   Chicago   Dallas   San Francisco
Toronto   London

REFRESHER COURSE IN GREGG SHORTHAND SIMPLIFIED

11 12 13 14 15 16 RM RM 9 8 7 6 5 4 3 2 1

ISBN 07-062248-5

Library of Congress Catalog Card No. 61-17346

Published by GREGG PUBLISHING DIVISION
McGraw-Hill Book Company, Inc.
Printed in the United States of America

ABOUT THIS BOOK

Have you taken a course in Gregg Shorthand (Simplified) in which you covered all the principles, yet because you've "been away from it" for a while, feel the need for a review? Then this book is for you. It is designed as a quick, yet thorough, review of Gregg Shorthand for those who have previously studied the system. If you have not had a complete course in Gregg, then this is *not* the book for you; you should study from a textbook that approaches the study of shorthand from the very beginning.

The purpose of this book is to review all the basic theory principles of the Gregg Shorthand system, to renew your knowledge of phrasing, to give you practice in writing shorthand that can be easily read (penmanship), and to "drive home" once and for all the brief forms that are so important in rapid writing.

THE BOOK IS ORGANIZED INTO 20 LESSONS

Lessons 1-15. Each of these lessons contains the following parts:

1. Know Your Alphabet. The better you know your alphabet, the more quickly you can construct outlines. This part of the lesson reviews for you the entire alphabet of Gregg Shorthand.

2. Proportion Drill. Whether you write large or small shorthand notes is unimportant. It is very important, however, that the proportion of your shorthand characters be accurate, so that you can tell instantly whether you meant an *a* or an *e*, an *r* or an *l*, an *s*, *p*, or *b*, and so on. The Proportion Drill will help you to write better shorthand—shorthand that is more easily transcribed.

3. Principles. A complete review of the basic principles of Gregg Shorthand is provided in this part through the medium of carefully organized charts of words and phrases.

4. Brief Forms and Phrases. This part of the lesson drills on the brief forms (all the brief forms in the Gregg system are presented), most-used phrases, and various special terms such as days of the week, months, and cities and states.

5. Reading and Self-Dictation Practice. The Reading and Self-Dictation Practice consists of letters or articles in shorthand that emphasize the shorthand devices presented in the first four parts of the

lesson. Your work with the shorthand in each Reading and Self-Dictation Practice will give you a further opportunity to speed up the relearning process; too, it will help you develop your shorthand writing speed.

The key to the Reading and Self-Dictation Practice exercises appears in the back of the book.

6. Don't Let This Happen to You. This special feature (appearing in Lessons 5, 10, 15, and 20) consists of examples of errors made by secretaries who misread their shorthand notes and failed to say what the dictator meant. Most of these errors came about because of poor proportion; others, because the stenographer did not use her head in selecting the right word.

Lessons 16-20. These lessons provide a further review of the principles in Gregg Shorthand, but in a different form. Each lesson concentrates on a major principle of the system, as follows:

Lesson 16 Brief Forms
Lesson 17 Joined Word Beginnings
Lesson 18 Joined Word Endings
Lesson 19 Disjoined Word Beginnings and Endings
Lesson 20 Omission of Vowels

In each lesson you will find:

1. *A review chart*
2. *A chart of 40 high-frequency words*
3. *A Reading and Self-Dictation Practice*

SUGGESTIONS FOR STUDY

Writing will always be easier if you READ aloud each section of the lesson first. Don't hesitate to use the key if you need it. You will probably use the key more frequently in the beginning lessons than you will in later ones.

Know Your Alphabet. Read the outlines as quickly as you can. Read them through a second time. After reading, write the outlines once in the order in which they are given, saying them aloud as you write them. Write them a second time.

Proportion Drill. Read the outline combinations and words before attempting to write them. Study the forms in order to see what is being emphasized in each drill—for example, *l* is about three times as large as *r; a* is huge, *e* is tiny. After reading and studying the proportion drill, make a shorthand copy of it. Compare your forms with those in the book; then, copy the drill again.

Principles. First read the brief explanation of the principles to be covered; then read the words across the columns, spelling any word you cannot immediately read. If after spelling you still cannot read a word, refer to the type key that appears below the drill. After reading the words across the columns, read down the columns. Try to check your reading time on each effort. When you have completed the readings, write each word twice, saying it aloud as you write.

Brief Forms, Phrases, and High-Frequency Words. Read the outlines across the columns; then, read down. Check with the key if necessary. Write each outline once, saying the word or phrase aloud as you write.

Reading and Self-Dictation Practice. Always *read* the shorthand material (using the key if necessary) *before* writing it. If possible, check your reading time on your first effort; repeat the reading, again checking your time. Then dictate the material to yourself (think of this process as "self-dictation" rather than mere copying) in this way:

1. Silently read a convenient group of words (perhaps eight or ten) from the printed shorthand.

2. Then "dictate" that group to yourself aloud, writing each word or phrase as you say it.

Don't Let This Happen to You. First, read what was dictated; then compare it with what was transcribed. You can readily see how the meaning can be changed by faulty proportion, lack of knowledge of the shorthand principles, or carelessness.

Concentrate on the principles of Gregg Shorthand and the development of good proportion in your notes during this part of your retraining program. If you do, you will find the next step — advanced dictation, speed development, and transcription — an easy transition.

Madeline S. Strony
M. Claudia Garvey
Howard L. Newhouse

LESSON 1

KNOW YOUR ALPHABET

k, g, r, l, n, m, t, d, h, th, a, e, i, o, u, s, f, v, s, p, b, sh, ch, j.

PROPORTION DRILL

Keep short strokes short, long strokes long. Make *a*'s huge, *e*'s tiny.

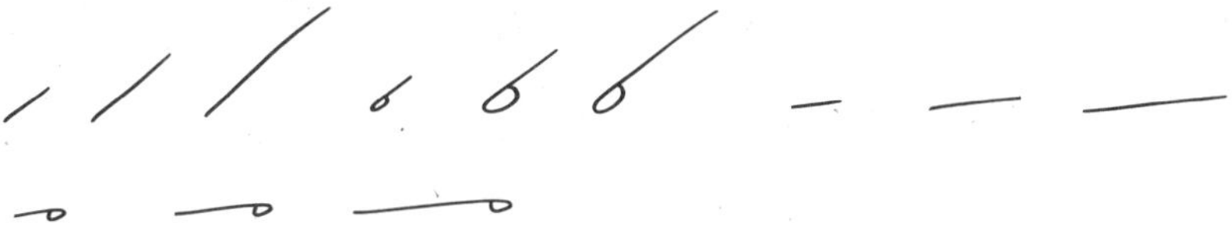

it-at, would, did-date, eat, add, added, in-not, am-more, men, any, me, many.

PRINCIPLES

Circle joinings.

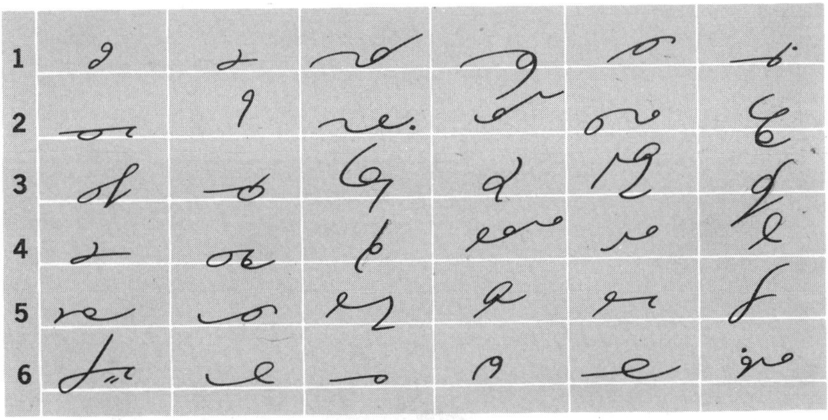

1. easy, seen, grade, gave, take, meeting.
2. names, each, clearing, reader, agree, prepare.
3. attached, might, branch, faces, driver, paved.

4. seem, answer, chip, territory, three, tax.
5. skill, lake, telephone, tire, teams, bath.
6. James, lax, me, these, mail, history.

BRIEF FORMS AND PHRASES

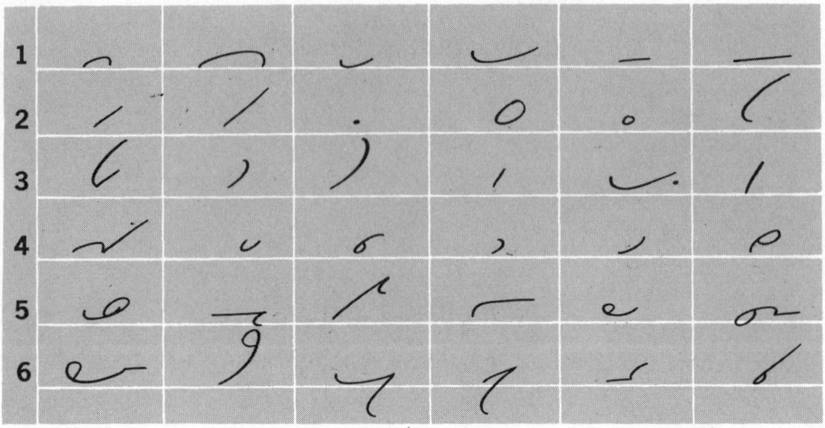

1. can, go-good, are-our-hour, will-well, in-not, am-more.
2. it-at, would, a-an, I, he, be-by.
3. but, for, have, shall-ship, willing, which.
4. could, of, with, is-his, their-there, that.
5. write-right, must, Dear Sir-desire, them, year-were, I cannot.
6. I will not, I have, will be, to be, in the, he would.

READING AND SELF-DICTATION PRACTICE

1. Mr. Hale:

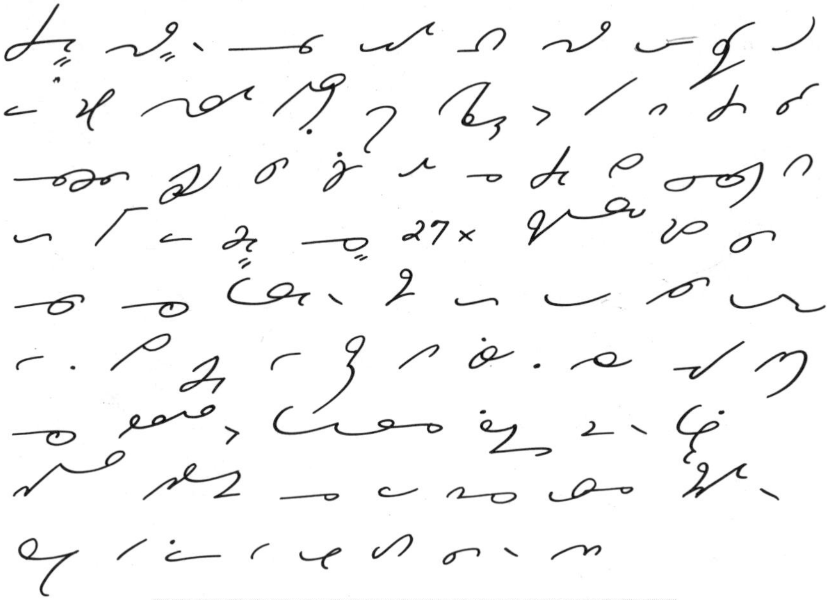

2. Dear Harry:

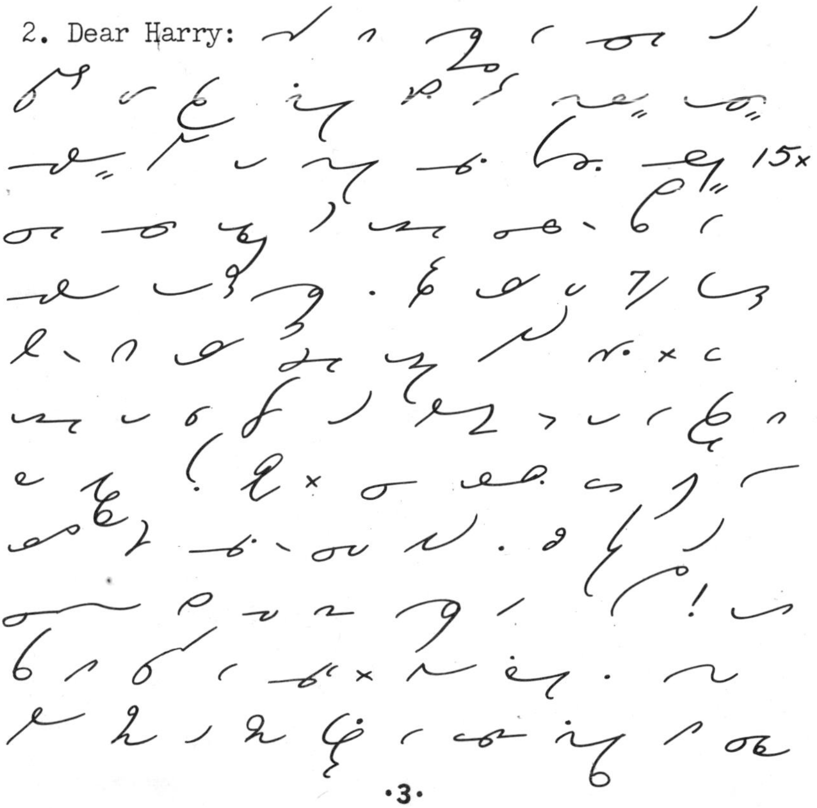

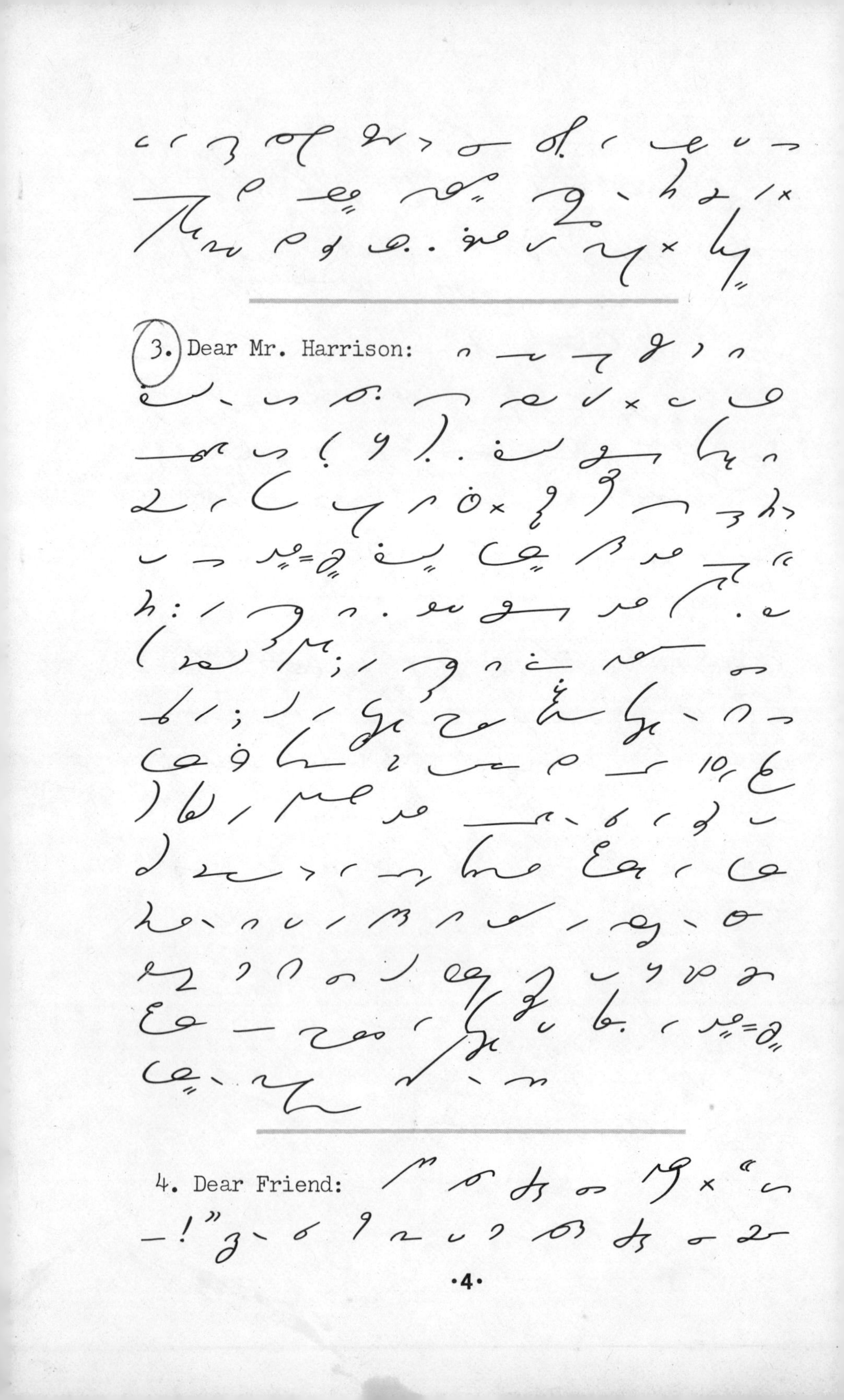

3. Dear Mr. Harrison:

4. Dear Friend:

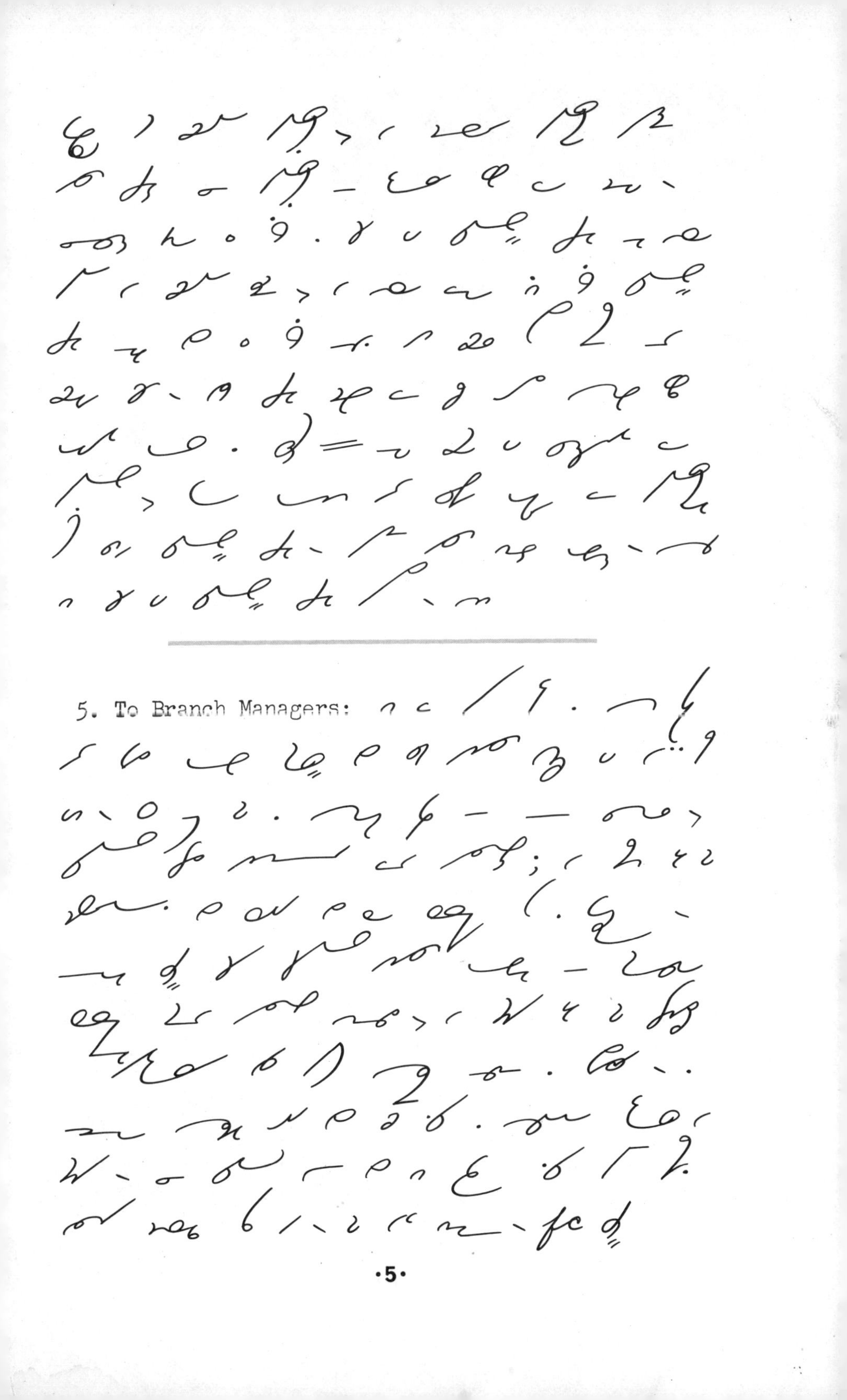

5. To Branch Managers:

LESSON 2

KNOW YOUR ALPHABET

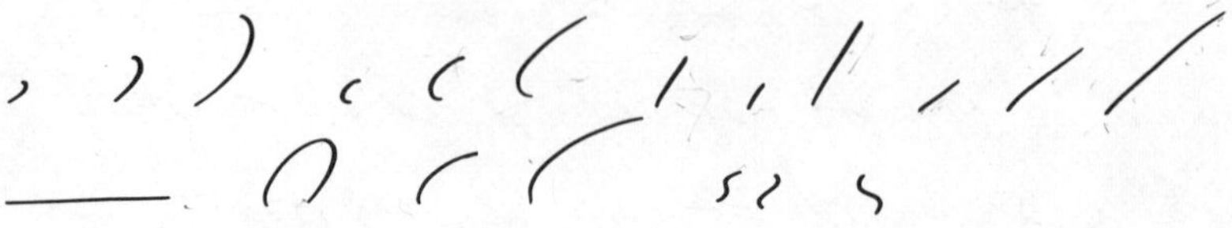

s, f, v, s, p, b, ch, sh, j, t, d, ted, men, tive, ten, dem, ses, xes.

PROPORTION DRILL

Keep hooks deep and narrow.

of, are, will, you, can, go, you, this, the, ten, time.

PRINCIPLES

Hook vowels; *w* in the body of words; *ses;* word beginning *ex;* word endings *sion-tion, tial.*

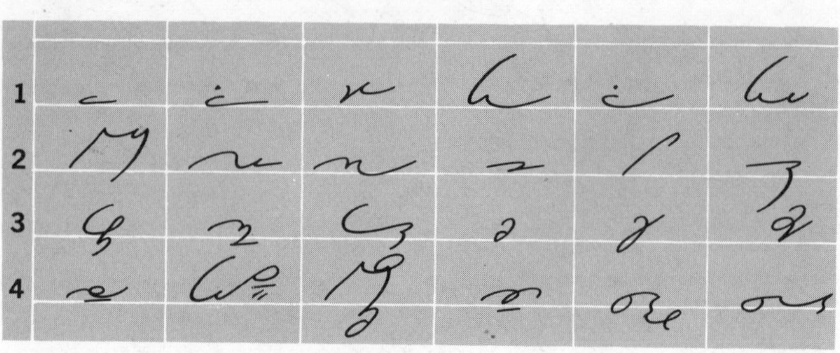

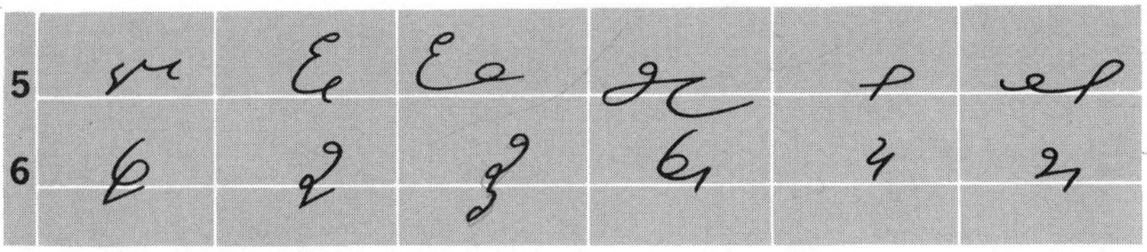

1. own, home, store, ball, whole, borrow.
2. drove, grown, cool, noon, do, move.
3. precious, cousin, plus, we, wait, waste.
4. queer, Broadway, driveway, quick, accessories, analysis.
5. sisters, express, explain, example, nation, relation.
6. patient, efficient, efficiency, partial, social, essential.

BRIEF FORMS, PHRASES, AND DAYS OF THE WEEK

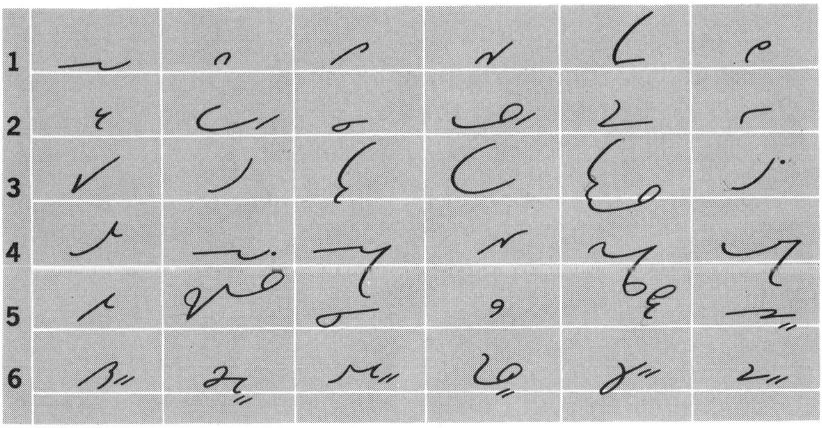

1. Mr.-market, you-your, to-too-two, yours truly, been, they.
2. was, pleased, when, liked, from, then-than.
3. should, and-end, business, bill, businesslike, ending.
4. ends, marketing, marketable, to the, you will be able, will not be.
5. it is, I should like, I am, he is, I was, Monday.
6. Tuesday, Wednesday, Thursday, Friday, Saturday, Sunday.

READING AND SELF-DICTATION PRACTICE

6. Dear Madam:

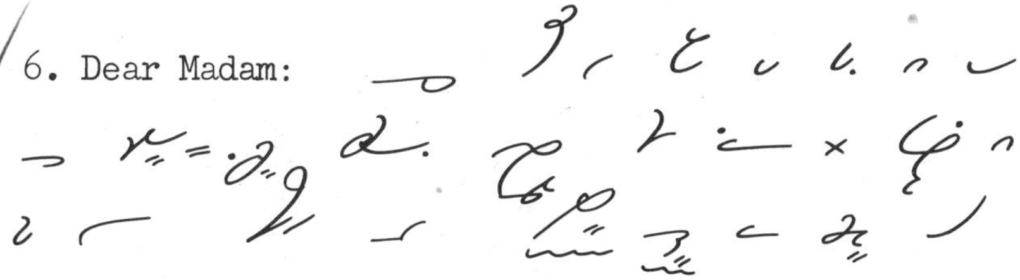

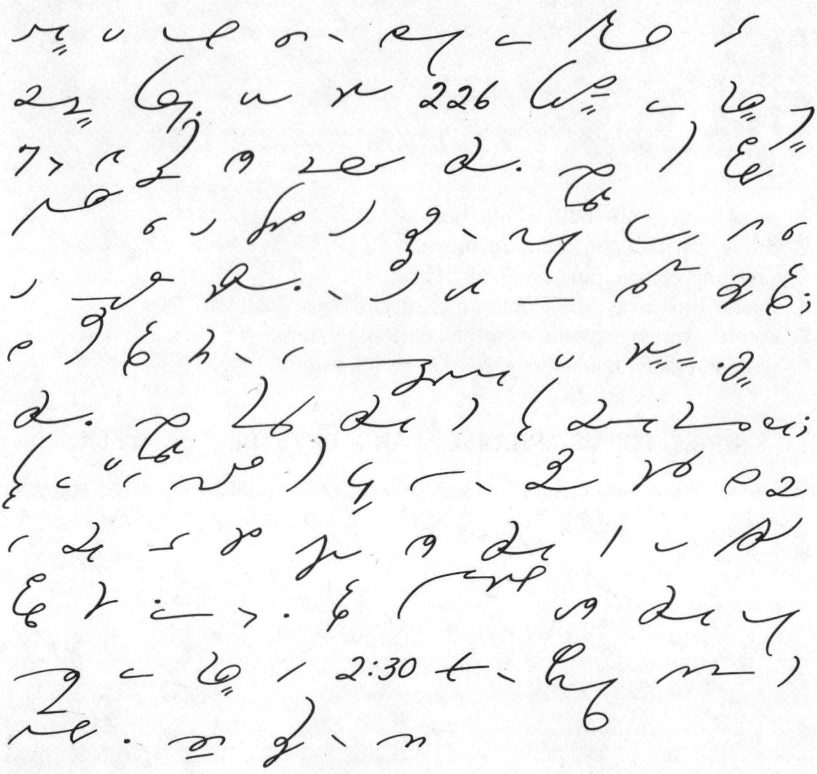

7. Dear Wade:

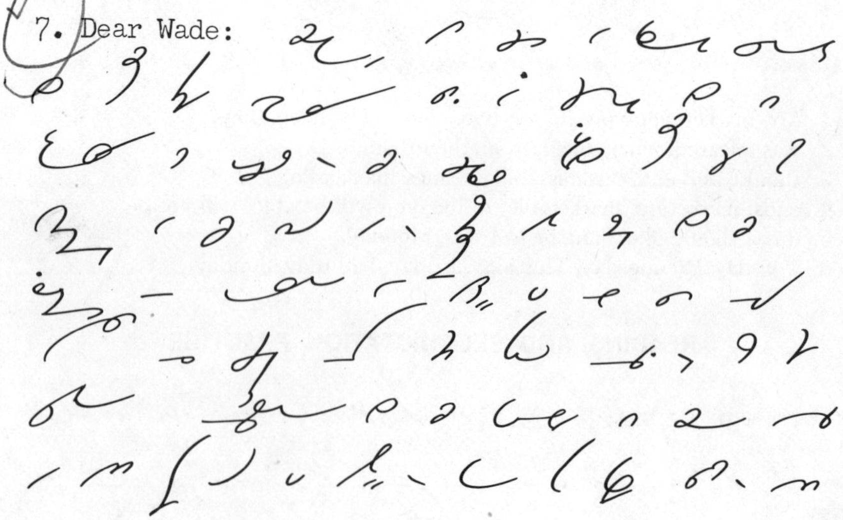

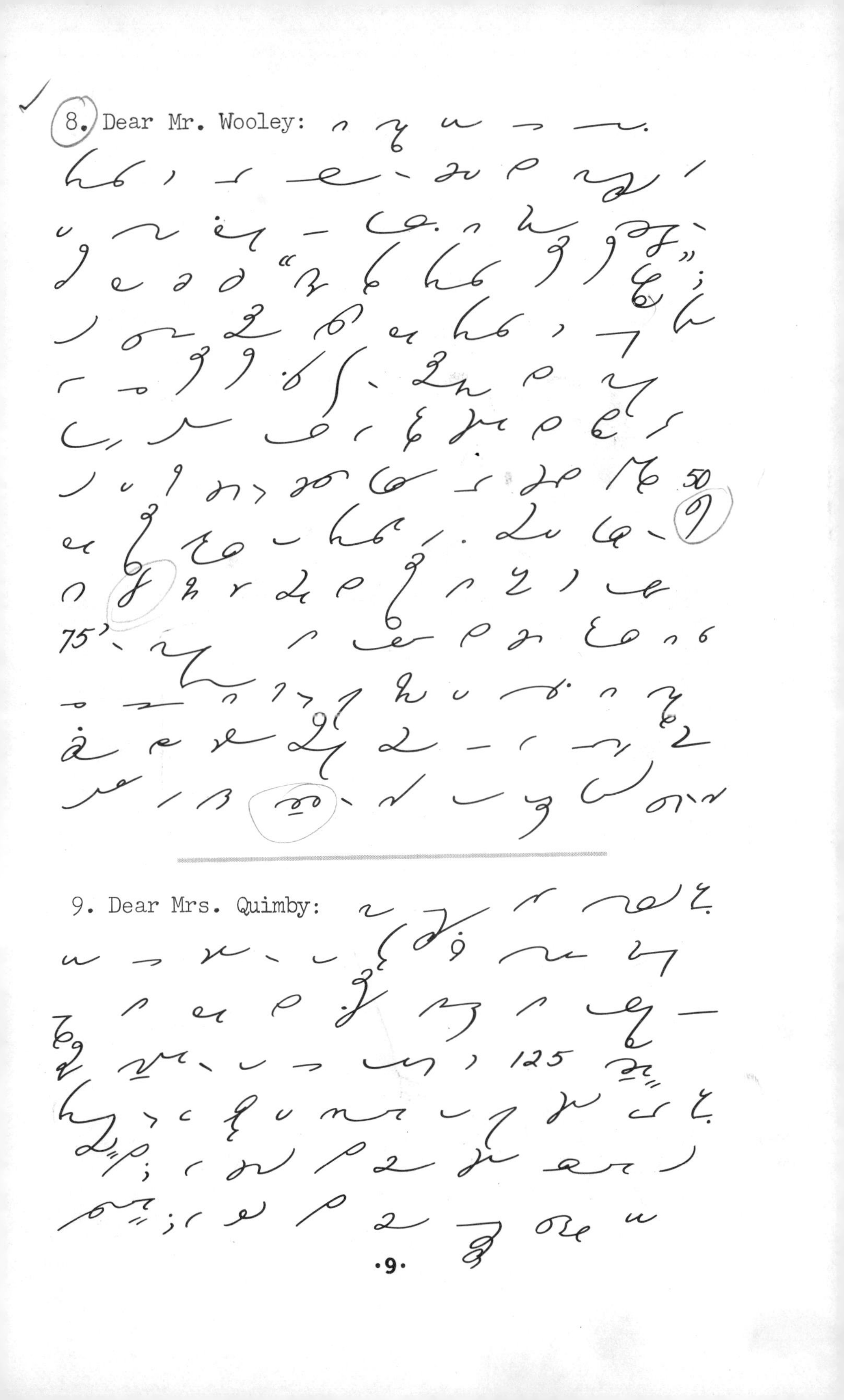

8. Dear Mr. Wooley:

50

75

9. Dear Mrs. Quimby:

125

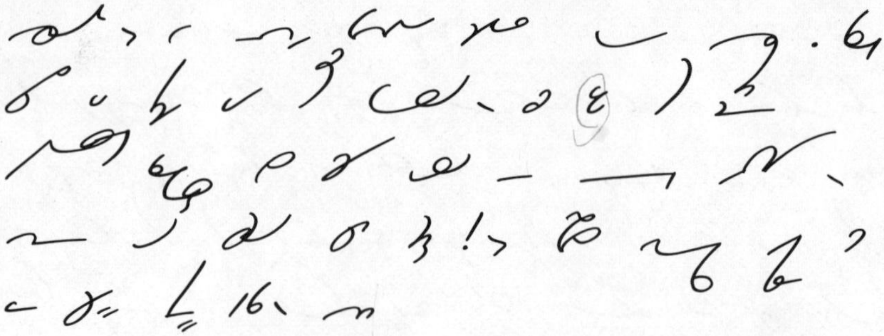

10. Dear Cousin Carol: 

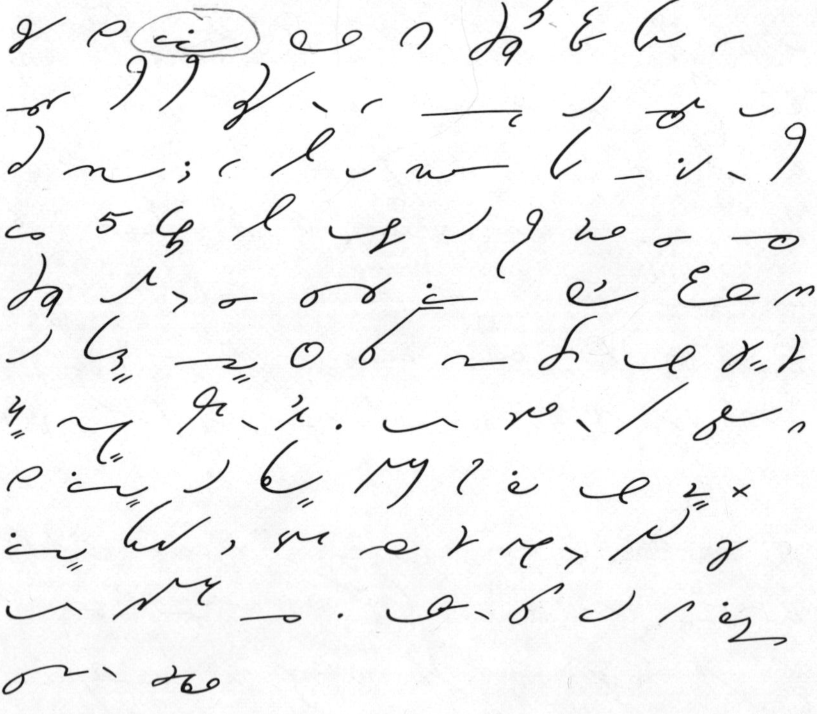

LESSON 3

KNOW YOUR ALPHABET

Notice the combinations of strokes.

k, r, kr, l, g, lg, kl, gr, gl, rk.

PROPORTION DRILL

Give *r* and *l* an upward turn at the finish. Write the *nt-nd, mt-md* blends upward from the line of writing.

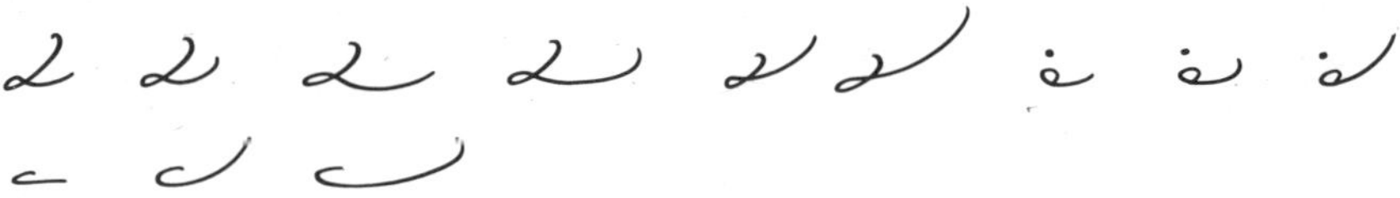

fear, feared, fill, filled, sent, seemed, hear, heard, hint, own, owned, old.

PRINCIPLES

Amounts; word beginnings *be, de, re, dis, mis;* word endings *ly, ily, ally; rd, ld.*

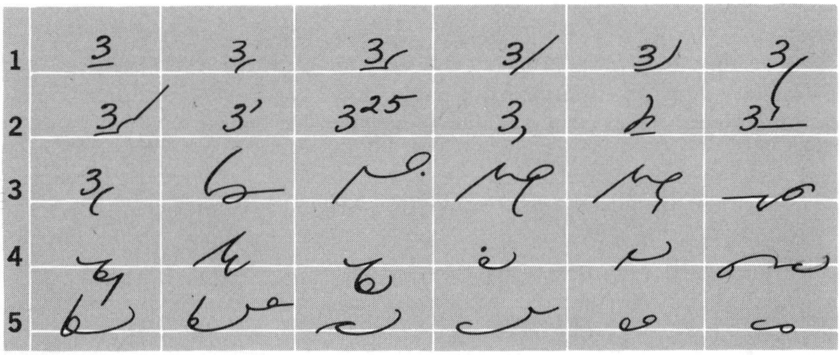

6 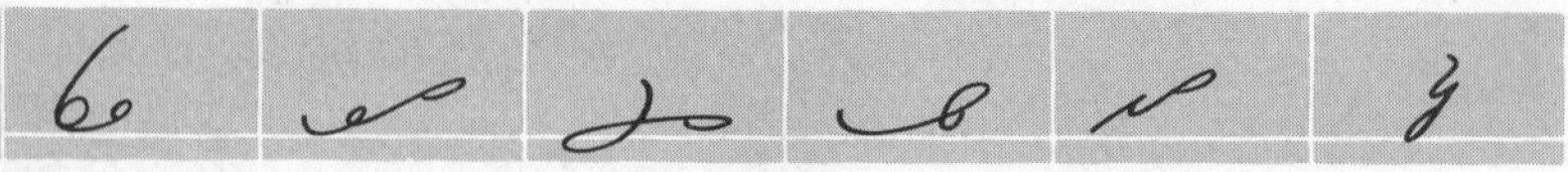

BUT

7 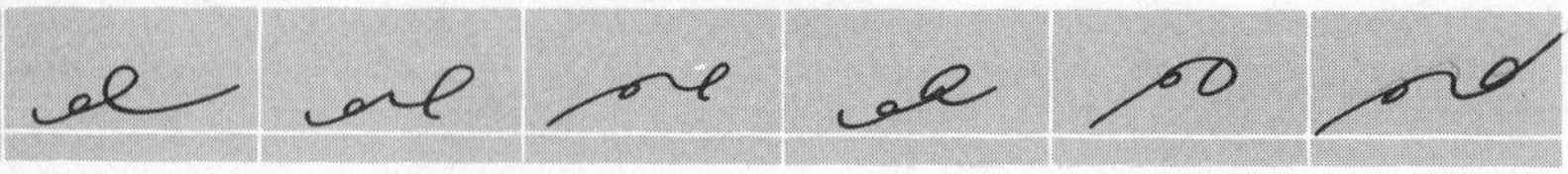

1. 300, 3,000, 300,000, $3, $300, 3 bushels.
2. $300,000, 3 cents, $3.25, 3 per cent, few hundred, 3 million.
3. 3 pounds, became, delaying, describe, description, mistake.
4. research, deposit, repaired, heard, toward, ignored.
5. child, children, cold, older, early, only.
6. barely, readily, family, likely, totally, socially.
   BUT
7. retail, retrace, decrease, retire, decay, degrade.

BRIEF FORMS, PHRASES, AND MONTHS

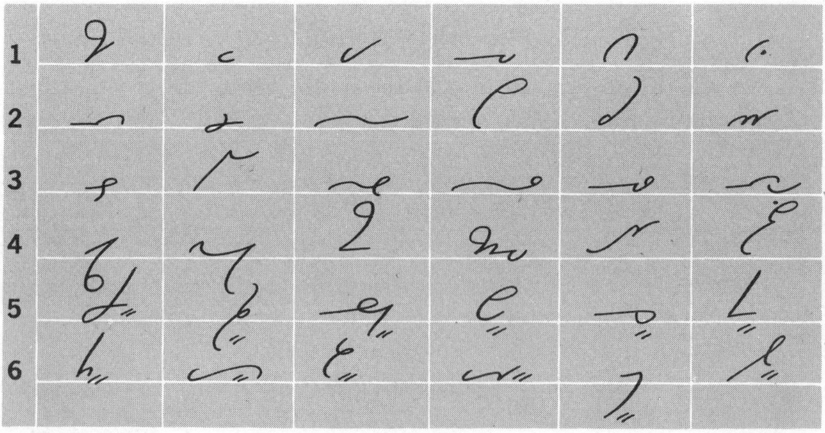

1. after, all, what, most, this, thing-think.
2. enclose, send, glad, about, very, worth.
3. necessary, doctor-during, correspond-correspondence, gladly, mostly, enclosure.
4. to be able, you will be, I have not, as you know, into the, has been.
5. January, February, March, April, May, June.
6. July, August, September, October, November, December.

READING AND SELF-DICTATION PRACTICE

11. Dear Mr. Field:

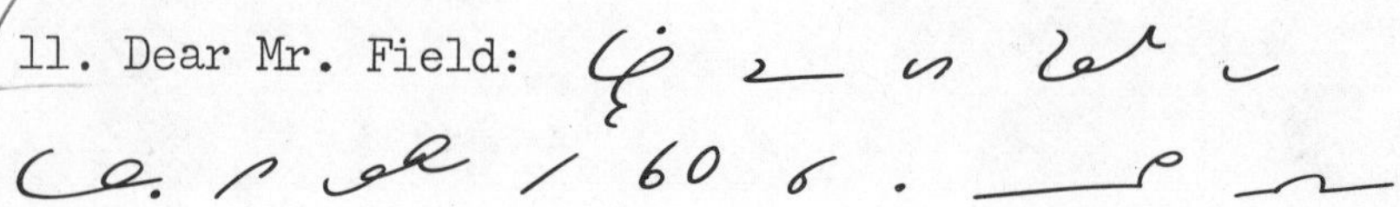

12. Dear Mr. Arnold:

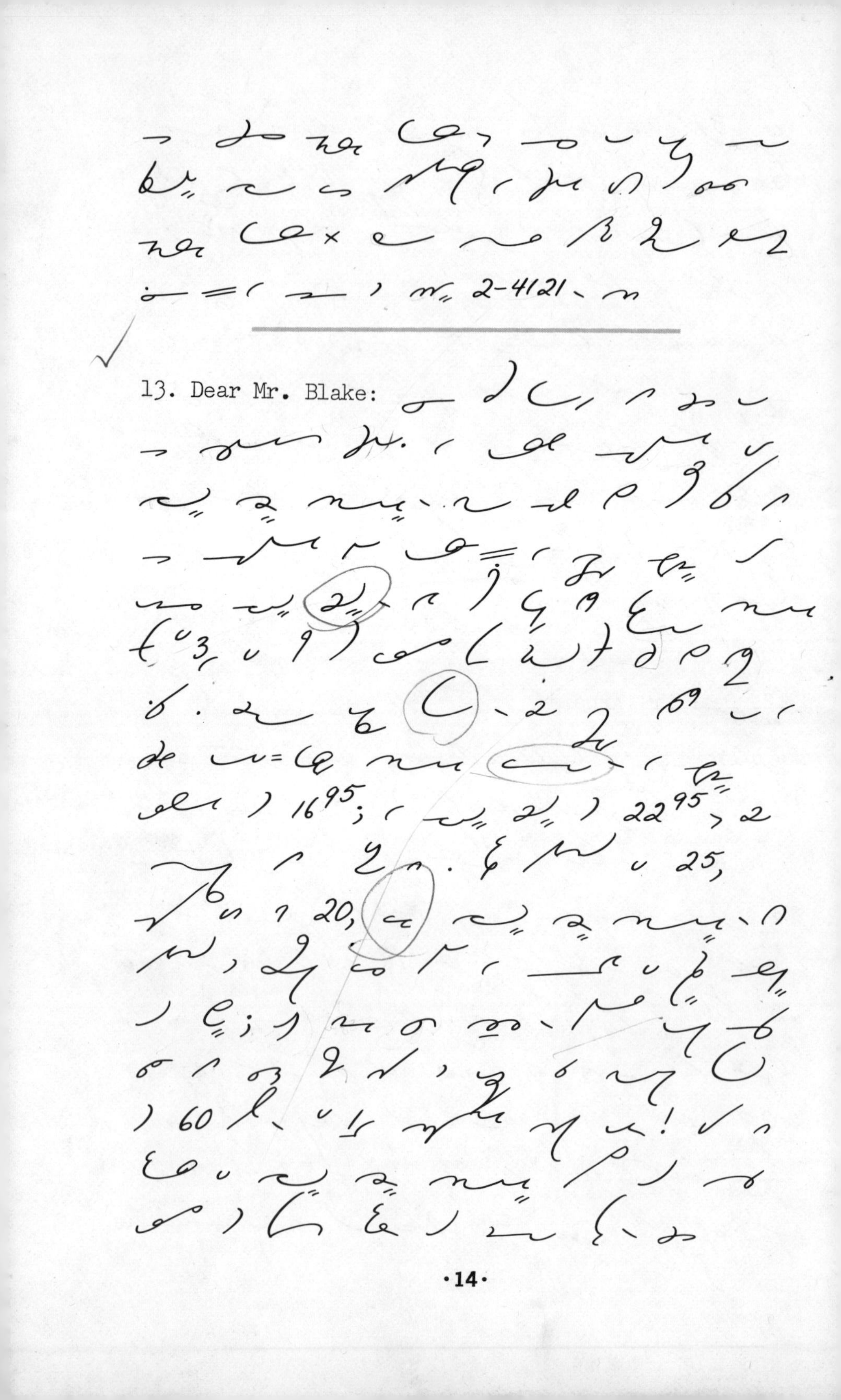

13. Dear Mr. Blake:

14. Dear Subscriber:

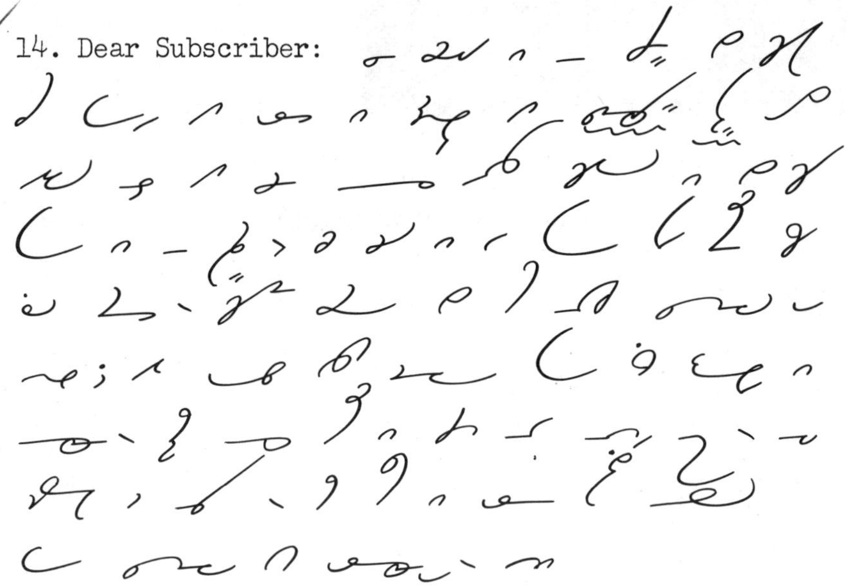

LESSON 4

KNOW YOUR ALPHABET

st, ts, ds, sn, ns, sns, sts.

PROPORTION DRILL

N and *m* are horizontal; *ng* and *nk* slant downward. Note that *nk* is longer than *ng*.

ban, bang, bank, brain, blame, blank, in, am, ink, seen, sing, sink.

PRINCIPLES

Word endings *ure, ture; ual, tual; ng, nk; y, ye, ya; aw, ah.*

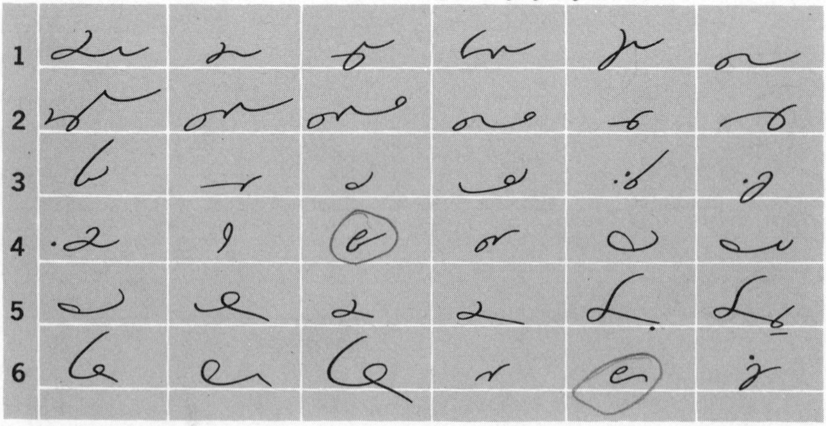

1. failure, secure, nature, picture, feature, equal.
2. schedule, actual, actually, equally, neither, gather.
3. bother, mother, either, leather, ahead, away.
4. aware, yes, yacht, youth, yard, yellow.

5. yield, rank, sing, sink, banking, banquet.
6. bring, along, blank, other, yoke, whether.

BRIEF FORMS, PHRASES, CITIES, AND STATES

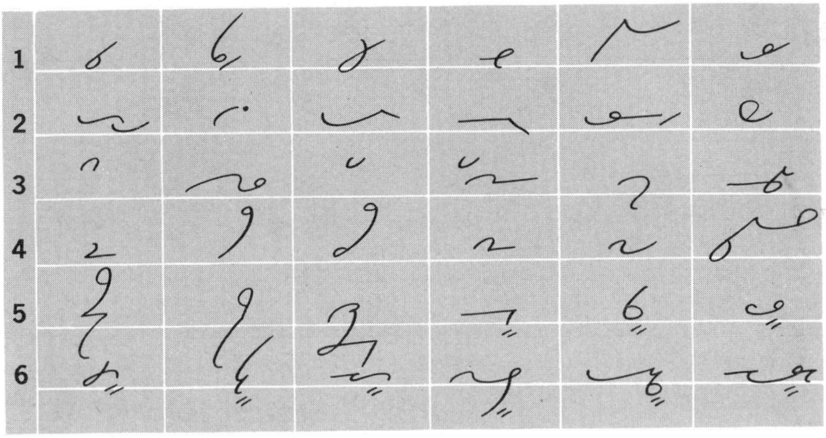

1. yet, believed, satisfy-satisfactory, next, deliver, return.
2. worker, thank, long, among, remitted, where.
3. under, greatly, over, overcome, keep-company, matters.
4. soon, ever, every, one, you are, I would like.
5. I have not been, I shall be, thank you very much, Michigan, Pennsylvania, Oregon.
6. Chicago, Boston, New York, Cleveland, Los Angeles, New Orleans.

READING AND SELF-DICTATION PRACTICE

15. Dear Mr. Franklin:

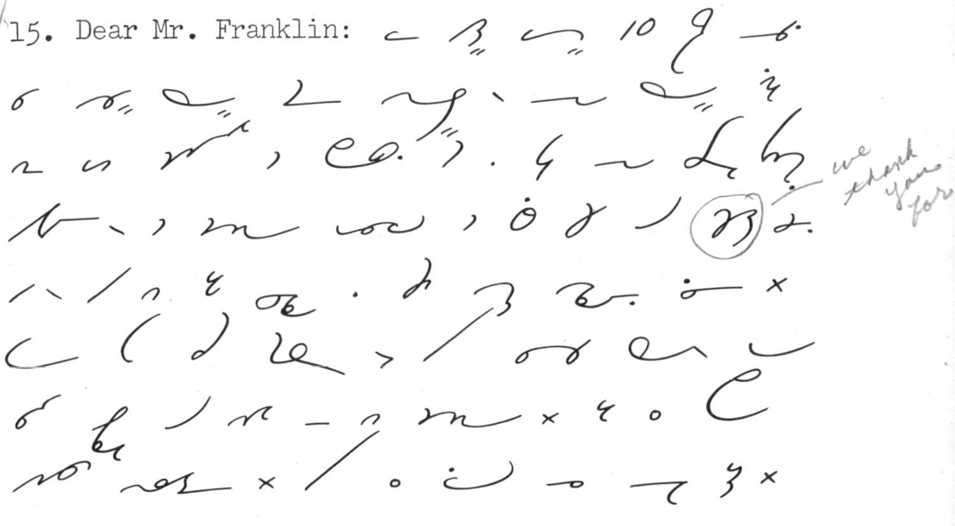

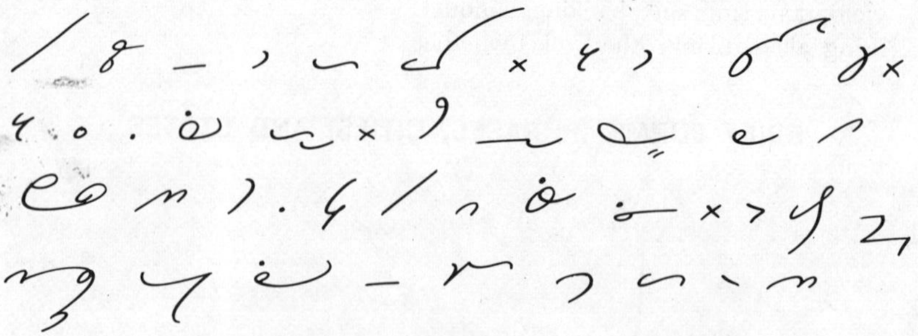

16. Dear Mr. White: 

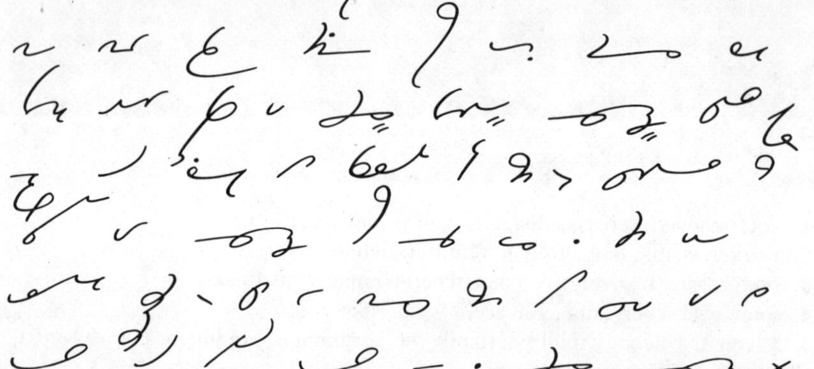

17. Dear Mrs. Jackson: 

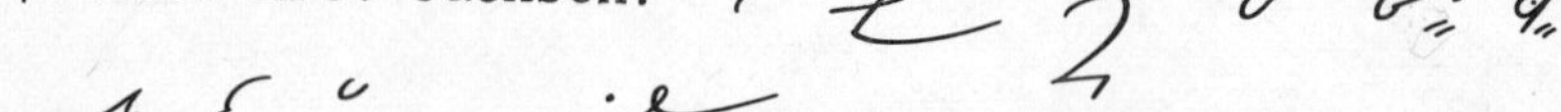

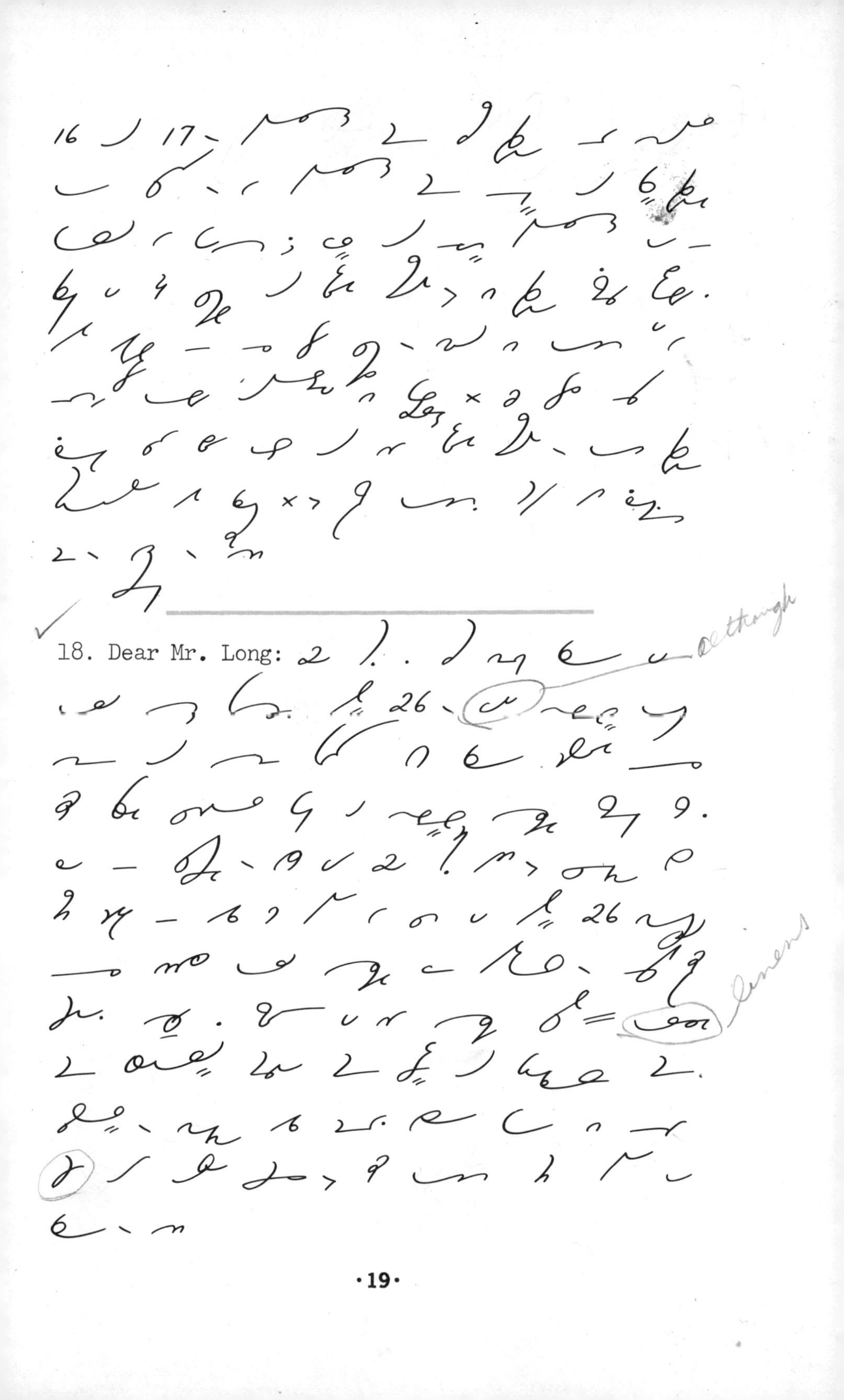

16 17

18. Dear Mr. Long: 26 26

LESSON 5

KNOW YOUR ALPHABET

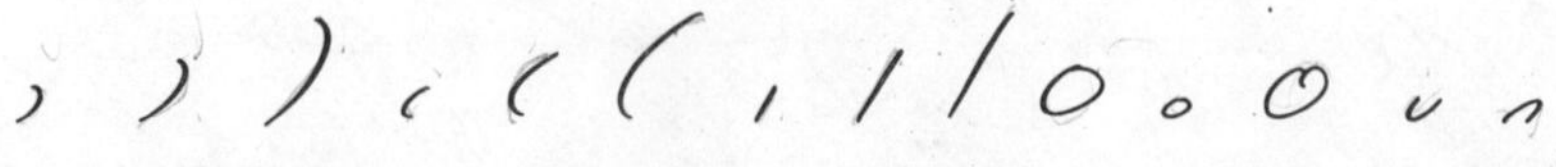

s, f, v, s, p, b, sh, ch, j, a, e, i, o, oo.

PROPORTION DRILL

S is a small curve; *oo* is a deep hook; *sh, ch,* and *j* are straight downstrokes.

see, say, we, way, several, we have, she is, chief, session, we shall, sage, wage.

PRINCIPLES

Blends *ten-den-tain, tem-dem;* omission of short *u;* omission of minor vowels; word endings *ment, able-ible.*

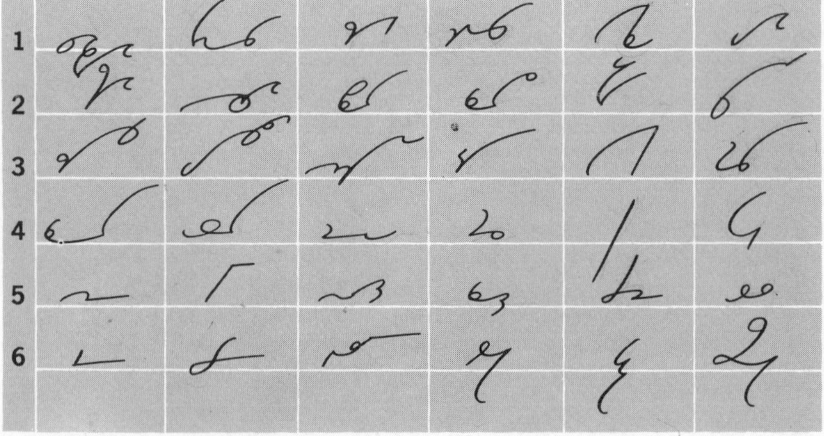

1. acceptance, bulletin, extension, straighten, danger, audience.
2. evidence, guidance, ascertain, certainly, obtain, attempt.
3. estimate, automatic, customer, system, damage, freedom.
4. seldom, random, summer, funny, judge, brush.
5. come, done, courteous, serious, genuine, theory.
6. shipment, payment, treatment, terrible, possible, available.

BRIEF FORMS AND PHRASES

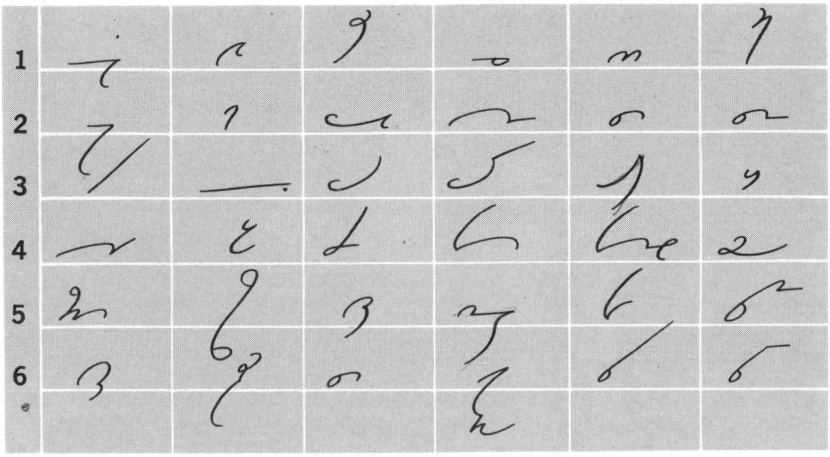

1. important-importance, those, several, any, world, suggest-suggestion.
2. unable, usual-wish, always, gone, weak-week, weaken.
3. did-date, morning, want, wanted, individual, office.
4. got, opportunity, general, big, bigness, we will.
5. if you can, I have been able, thank you for, you must have, by the, I do not.
6. this is, we shall be, he can, to be sure, he did, he would not.

READING AND SELF-DICTATION PRACTICE

19. Dear Mr. Weeks:

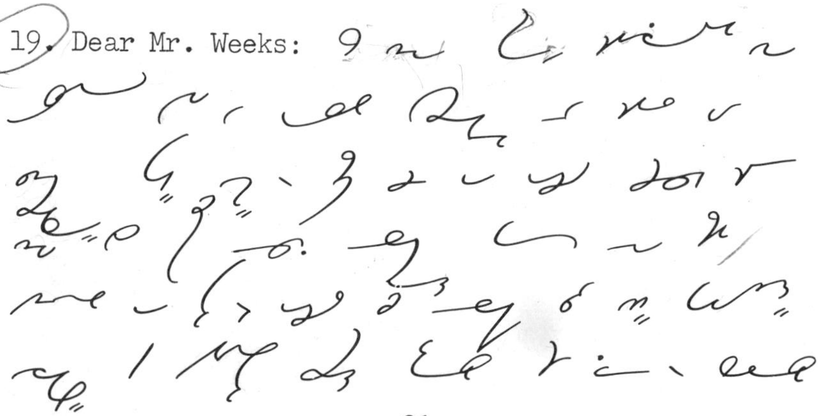

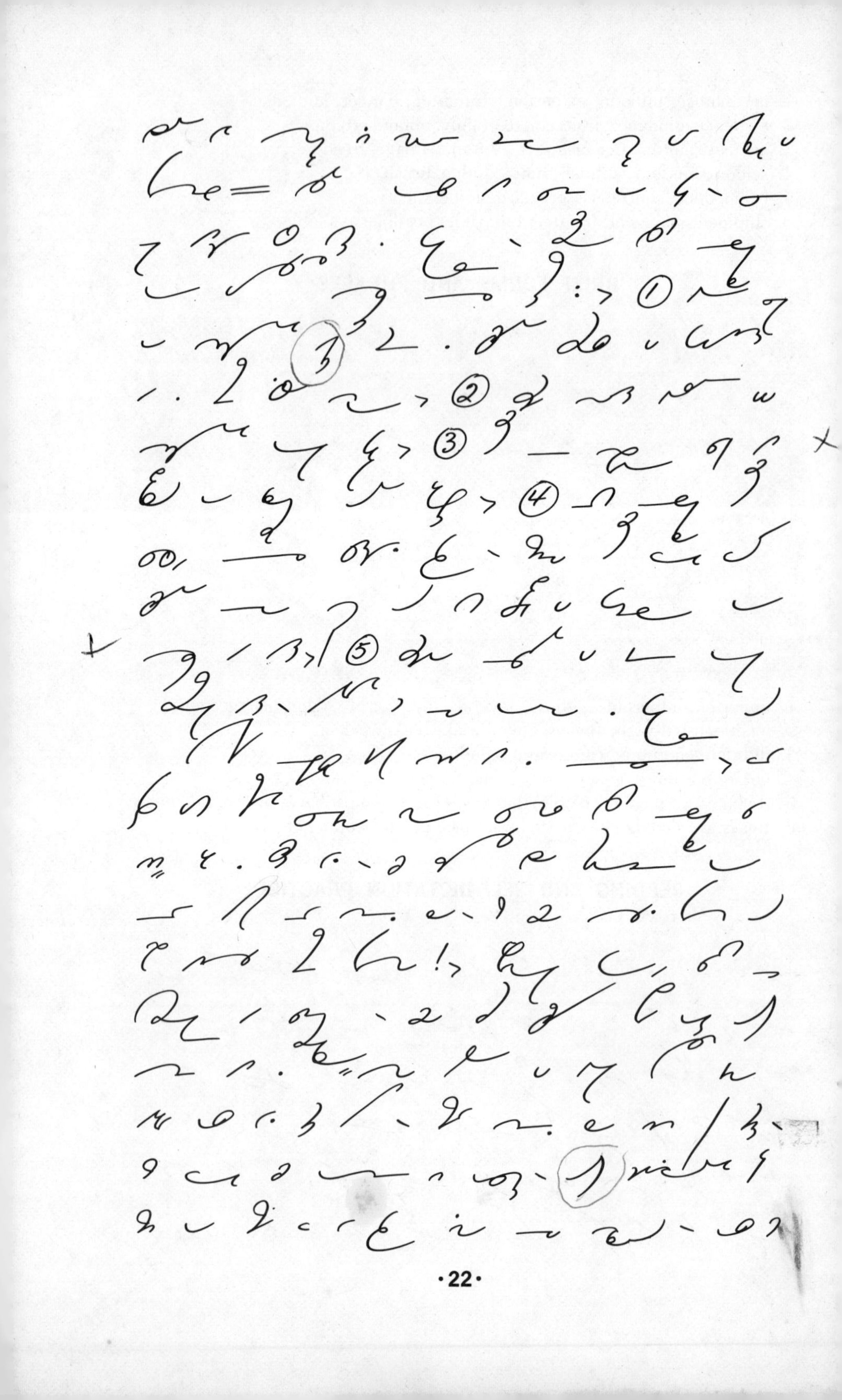

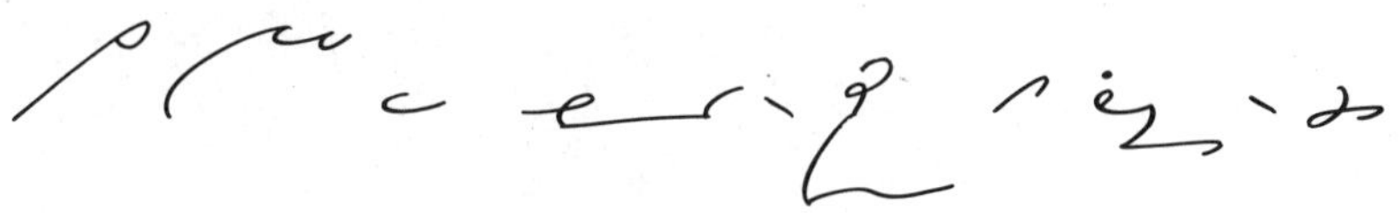

20. Dear Mrs. Swift:

21. Dear Mrs. Lane:

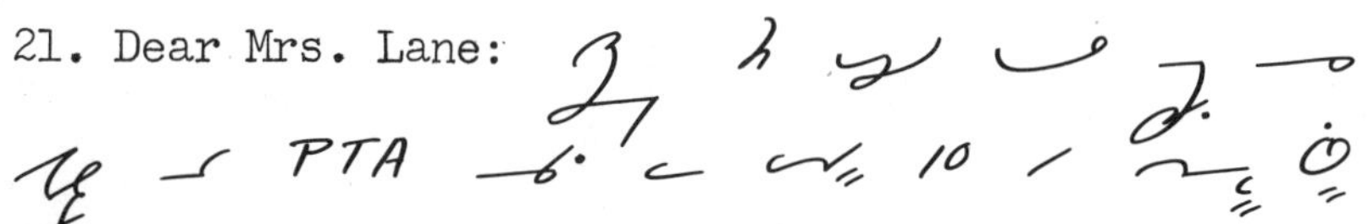

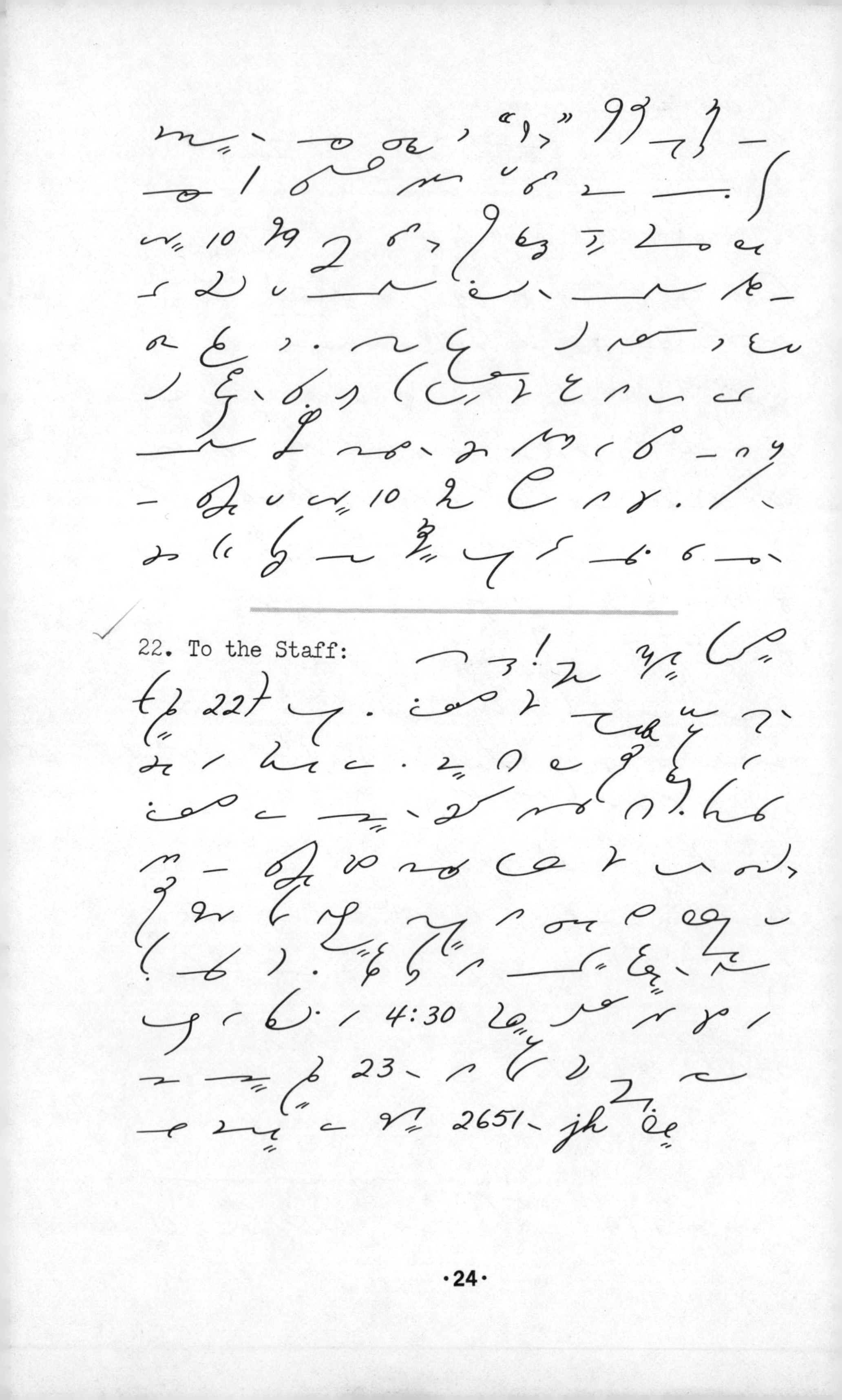

22. To the Staff:

DON'T LET THIS HAPPEN TO YOU!

DICTATED

1. He *did* not keep the materials in order.

2. *This* can be finished in an hour.

3. He will not *bother* you with the details.

4. We *order* our goods every week.

TRANSCRIBED

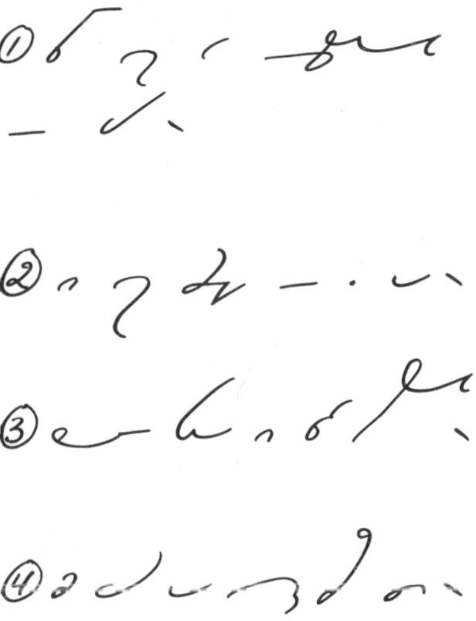

1. He *would* not keep the materials in order.

2. *You* can be finished in an hour.

3. He will not *bore* you with the details.

4. We *want* our goods every week.

LESSON 6

KNOW YOUR ALPHABET

a, e, i, ī a, ĭ a, o, oo, u, ow.

PROPORTION DRILL

known, noon, core, coal, cool, bone, boon, shows, choose, shore, sure.

PRINCIPLES

The sounds of *oi, ū, ow;* blends *ted-ded-det, men-mem, nt-nd, mt-md.*

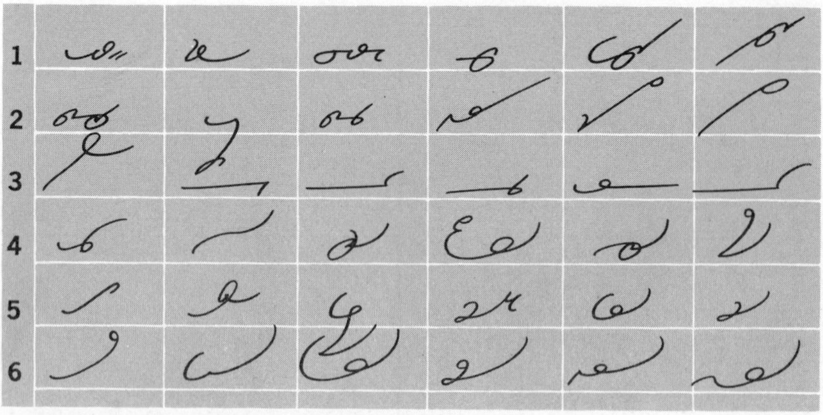

1. Roy, soil, annoyance, now, proud, doubt.
2. unite, review, unit, treated, study, today.
3. detail, mention, month, minute, remain, maintain.
4. retain, tenant, signed, explained, kind, event.
5. into, entire, prevent, windows, print, sent.
6. empty, prompt, blamed, exempt, trimmed, claimed.

BRIEF FORMS, PHRASES, CITIES, AND STATES

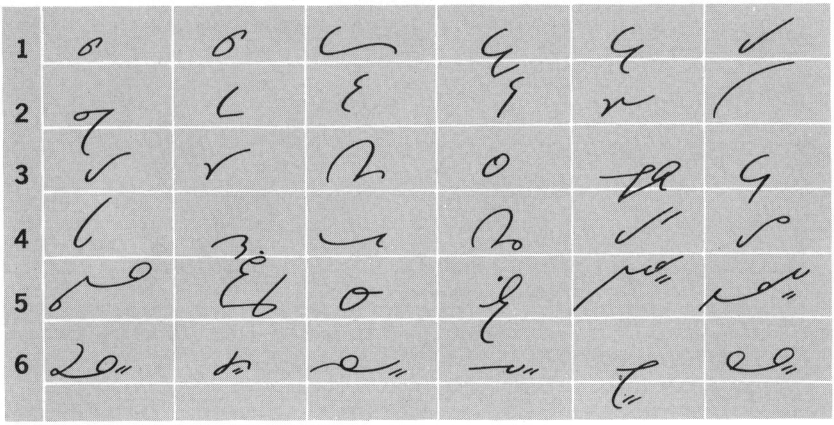

1. use, out-how, progress, property, purpose, order.
2. enable, upon, speak, such, street, time.
3. ordinary, stand, difficult, why, merchandise, purchase.
4. body, consider, else, difficulty, ordered, ordinarily.
5. he would like, has been made, why not, there has been, Detroit, Toledo.
6. Philadelphia, Chicago, California, Missouri, Nebraska, Alabama.

READING AND SELF-DICTATION PRACTICE

23. Dear Mr. Royal:

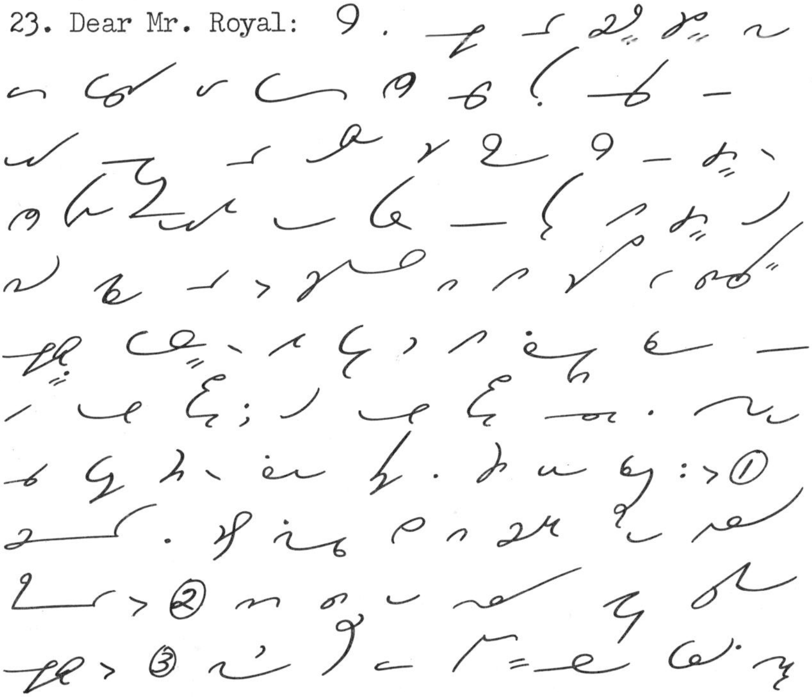

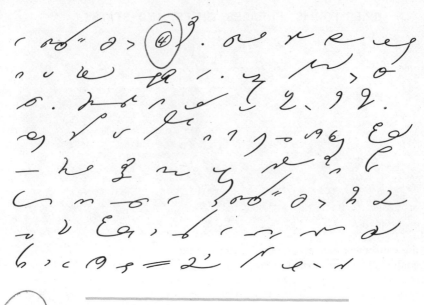

24. Dear Mr. Conant:

25. Dear Roy:

26. Dear Mr. Temple:

LESSON 7

KNOW YOUR ALPHABET

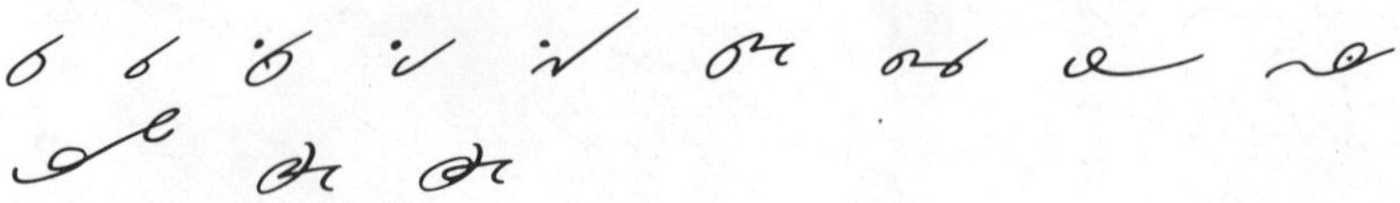

ate, eat, height, hot, hood, ounce, unit, oil, create, radio, signs, science.

PROPORTION DRILL

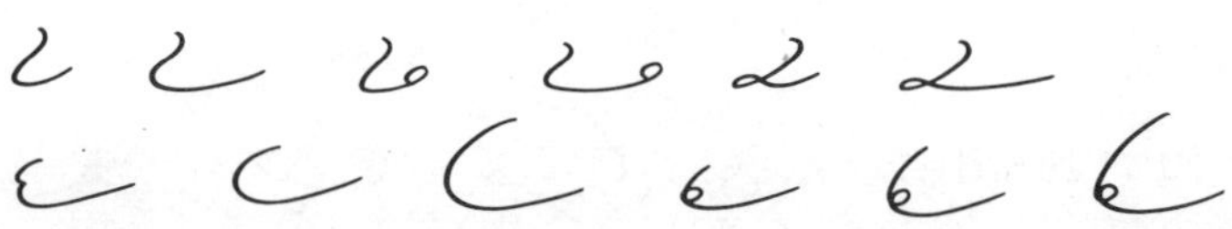

fr, fl, free, flee, fear, feel, sl, pl, bl, sell, peel, bell.

PRINCIPLES

Vowel combinations *īa, ēa, ĭo;* omission of *ow* before *n;* omission of vowel in *ition-ation;* omission of *r;* word beginnings *per, pro.*

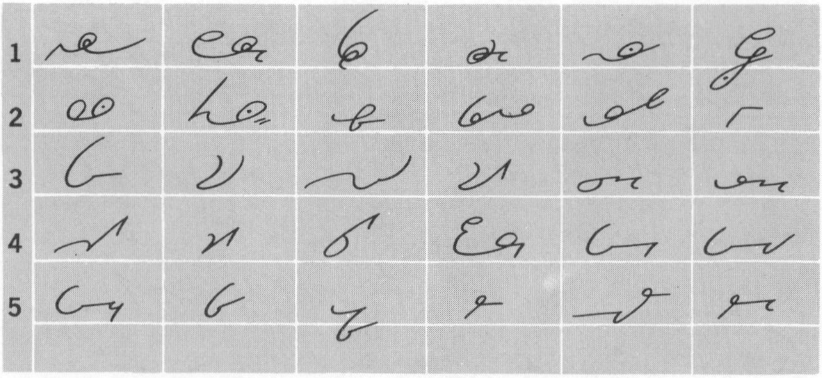

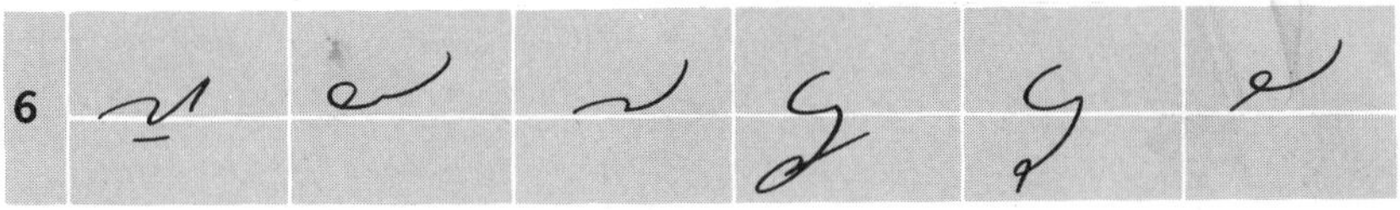

BUT

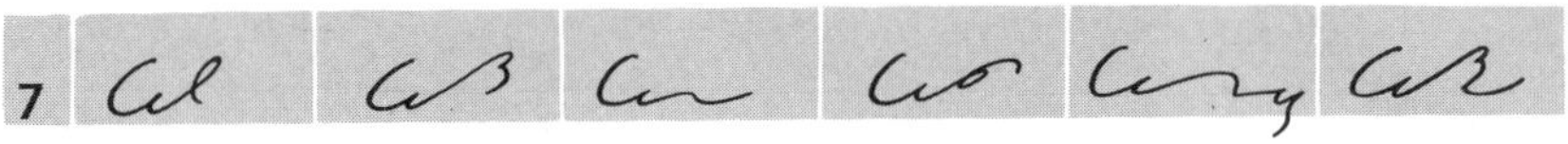

1. trial, appliance, bias, science, create, appreciate.
2. area, Julia, rayon, poetry, radio, town.
3. brown, found, ground, foundation, announce, renounce.
4. condition, station, addition, explanation, permission, promote.
5. promotion, port, report, turn, modern, terms.
6. quotation, around, count, provide, provision, turned.
   BUT
7. protest, produce, procure, protect, prognosis, producer.

BRIEF FORMS AND COMPOUNDS

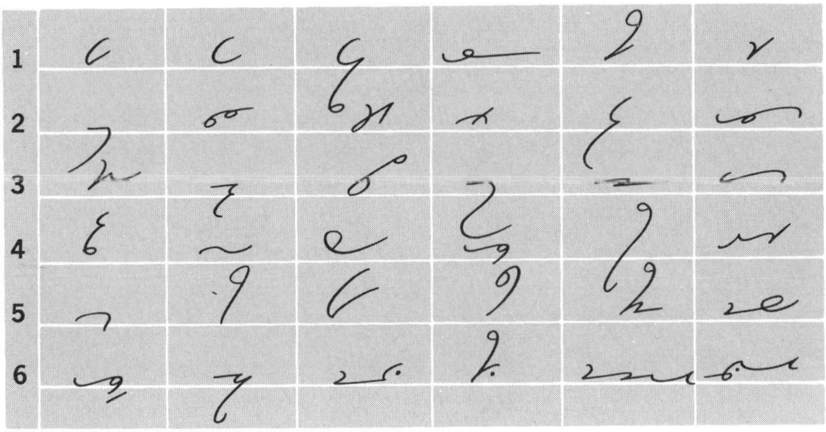

1. part, present, probably, remember, advertise, state.
2. never, within, situation, quantity, public-publish, regular.
3. future, newspaper, idea, envelope-nevertheless, number, organize.
4. experience, correct, allow, request, everybody, throughout.
5. question, agent, between, however, everyone, somewhere.
6. requested, nobody, something, everything, someone else, anything else.

READING AND SELF-DICTATION PRACTICE

27. Dear Mr. Brown:

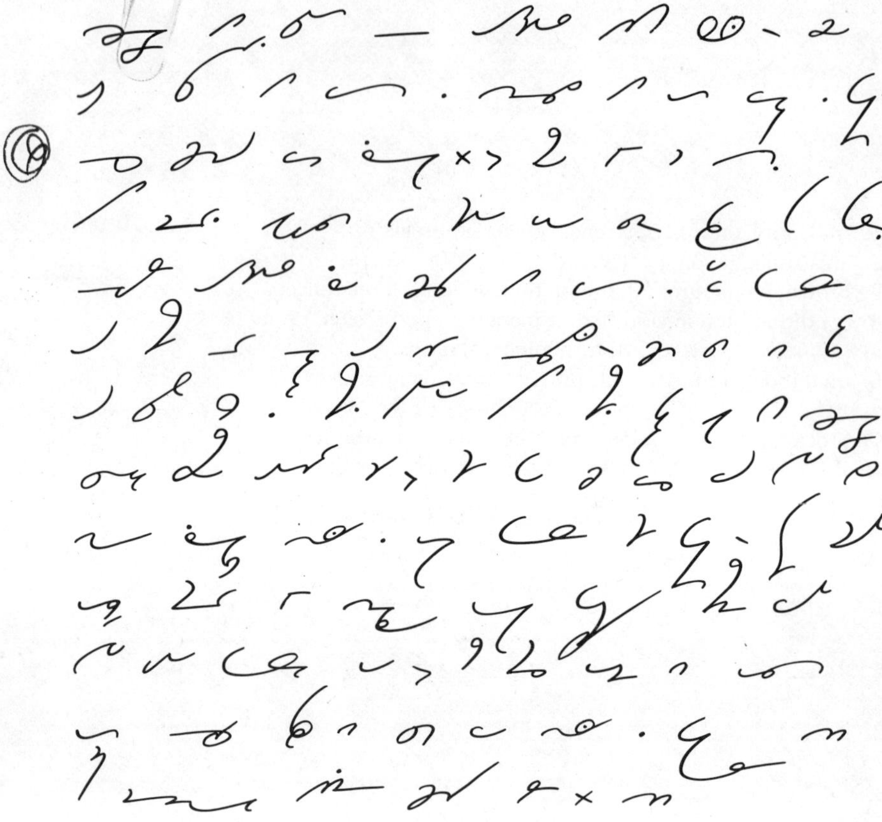

28. To the Staff:

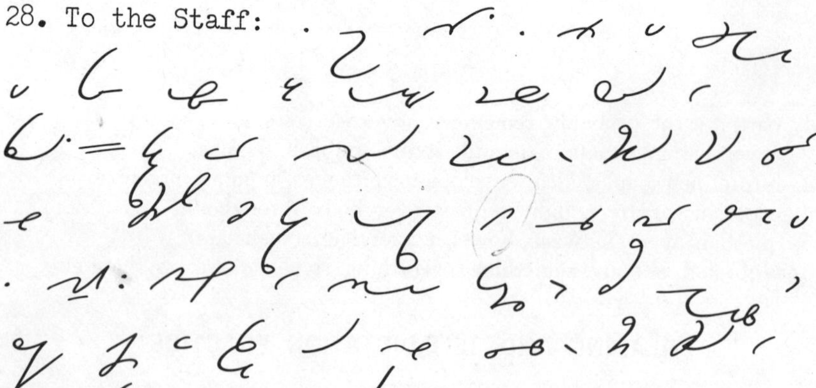

29. Dear Miss Porter:

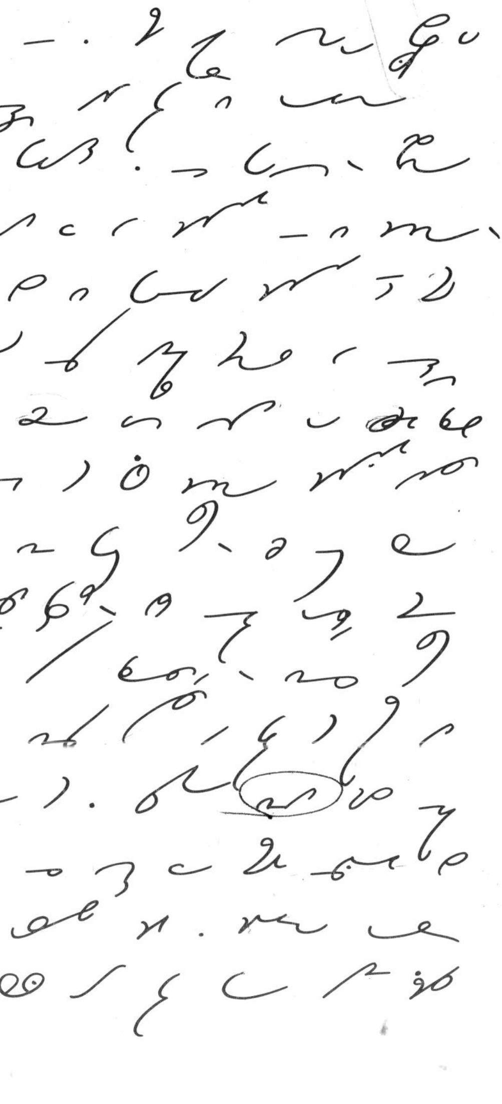

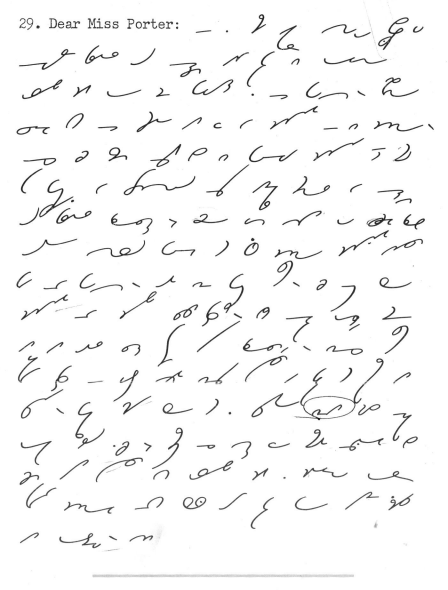

30. Dear Miss Field:

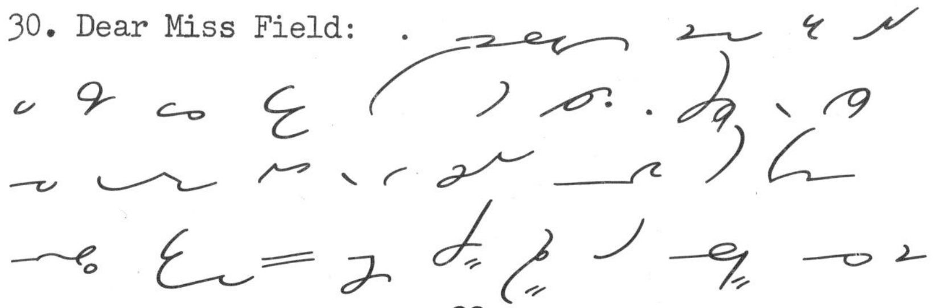

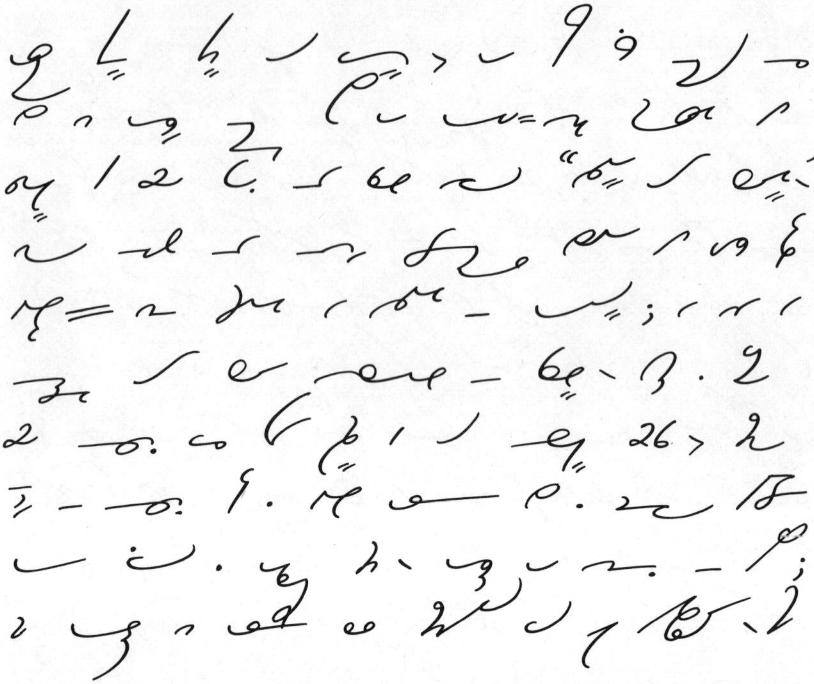

LESSON 8

KNOW YOUR ALPHABET

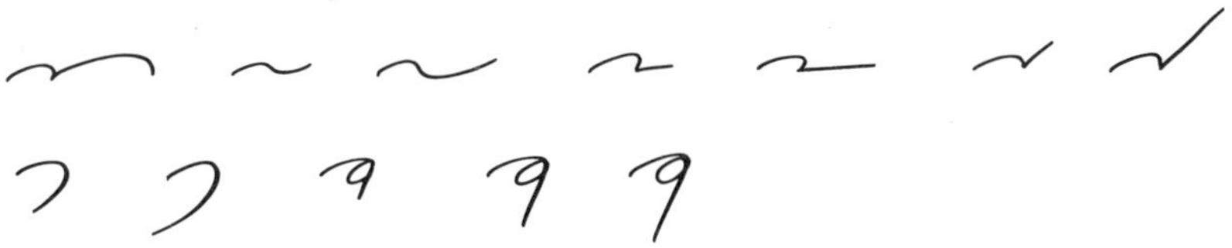

kg, kr, kl, kn, km, kt, kd, kf, kv, kash, kach, kaj.

PROPORTION DRILL

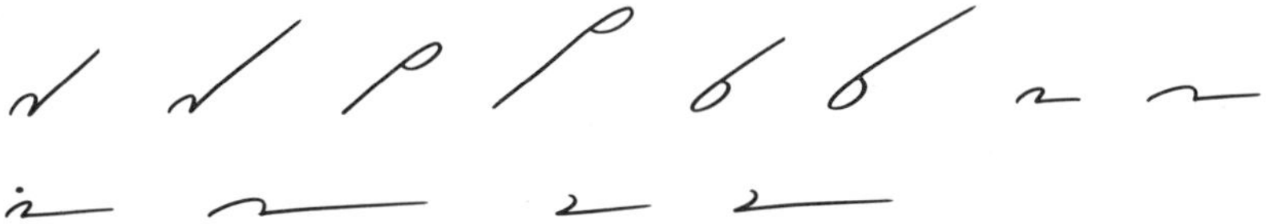

you would, you did, day, today, aid, aided, one, come, whom, common, some, summon.

PRINCIPLES

Word endings *ings, ingly, less, pose, position;* word beginnings *con, com, en, in, un, em, im, for, fore, fur.*

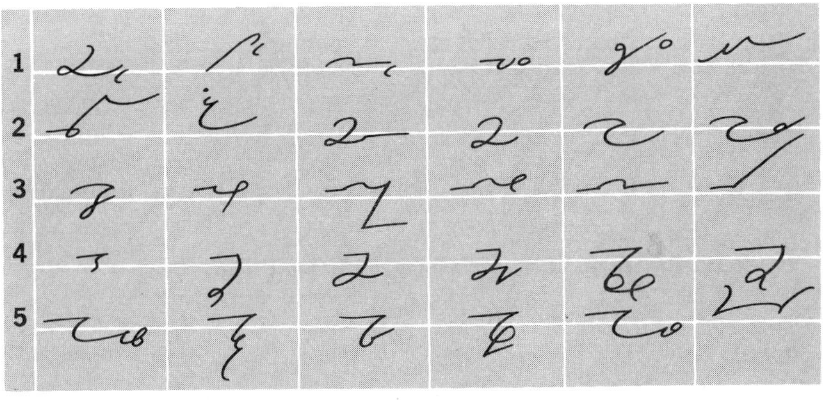

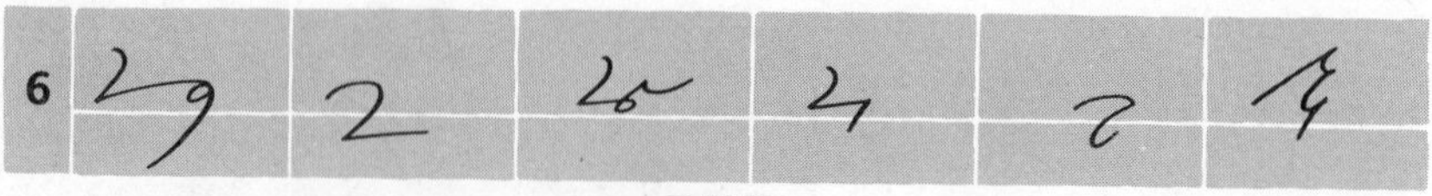

BUT

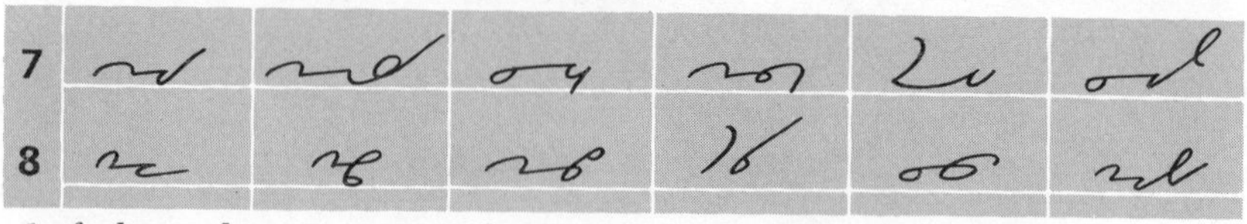

1. feelings, doings, comings, knowingly, exceedingly, thoughtless.
2. needless, hopeless, confirm, confer, compel, complete.
3. compete, enrich, encouragement, increase, income, indeed.
4. insist, invest, unfair, unfinished, embarrass, emphasis.
5. employee, impossible, import, impatient, employ, forgotten.
6. forgive, conform, furniture, furnish, compose, disposition.
   BUT
7. connote, comrade, emotion, connection, furlough, immodest.
8. unknown, uneasy, committee, forehead, enact, unnoticed.

BRIEF FORMS, PHRASES, CITIES, AND STATES

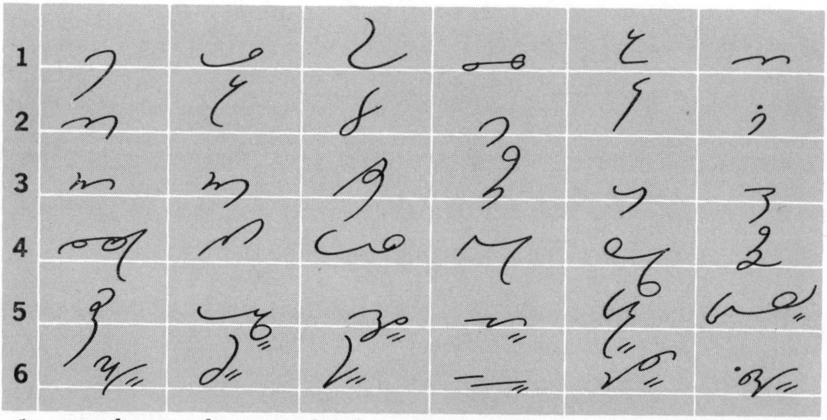

1. cover, letter, value, immediately, opinion, conclude.
2. conclusion, object, particular, confident-confidence, subject, house.
3. success, successful, disadvantage, advantageous, refer-reference, enough.
4. they might be, to this, please write, it will be, I will be able, if we are.
5. we shall have, Los Angeles, Kansas City, New York, Pittsburgh, Portland.
6. Washington, Virginia, Vermont, New Mexico, South Dakota, Houston.

READING AND SELF-DICTATION PRACTICE

31. Dear Mrs. Washington: 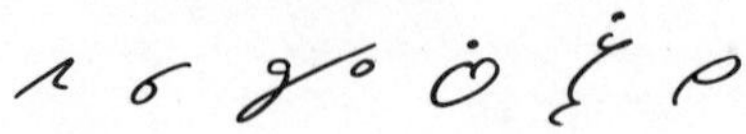

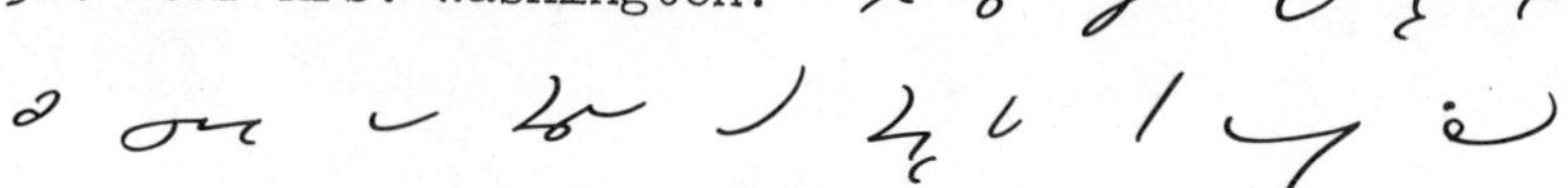

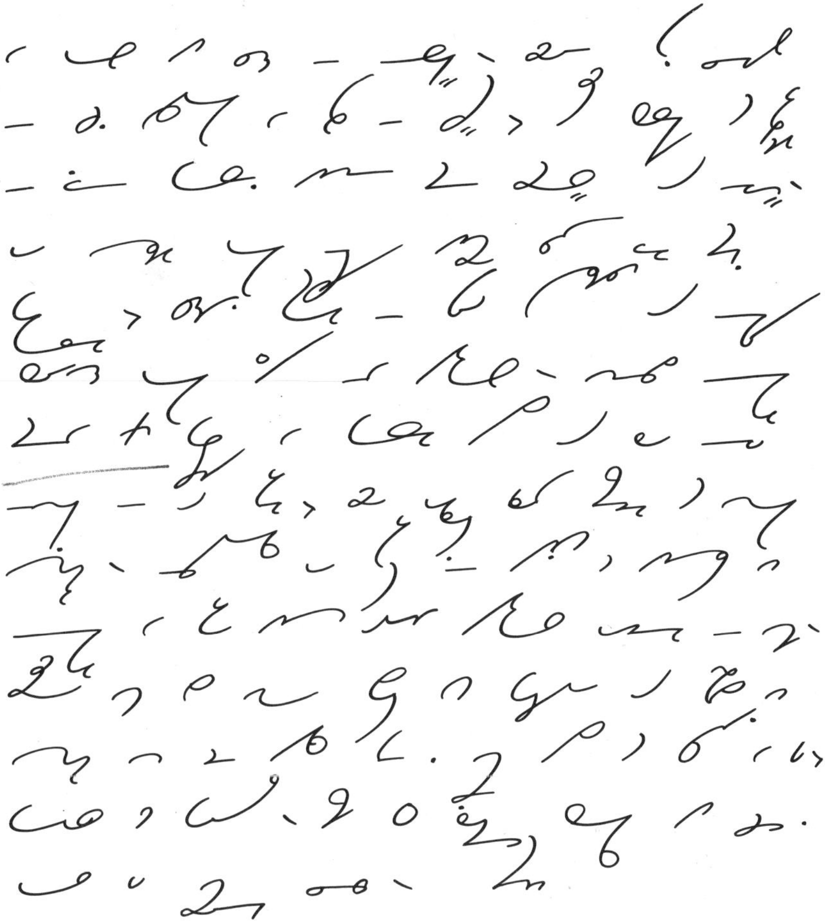

32. To Plant Managers in Houston, Los Angeles, and Portland:

33. Dear Mr. Conrad:

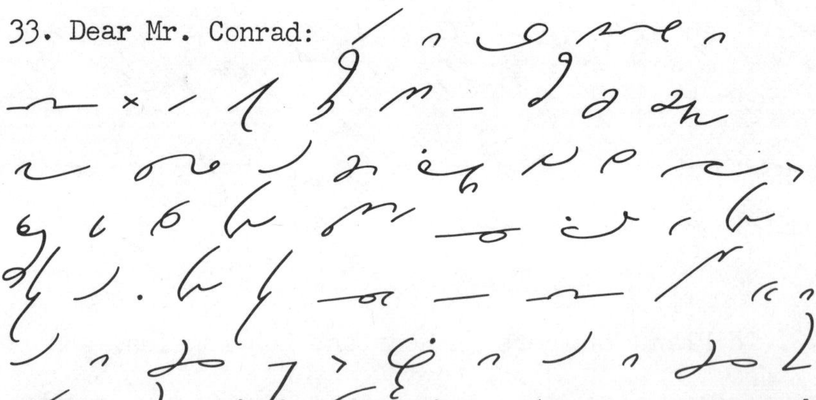

LESSON 9

KNOW YOUR ALPHABET

k, th, ten, tem, r, th, nd, md, r, rd, l, ld.

PROPORTION DRILL

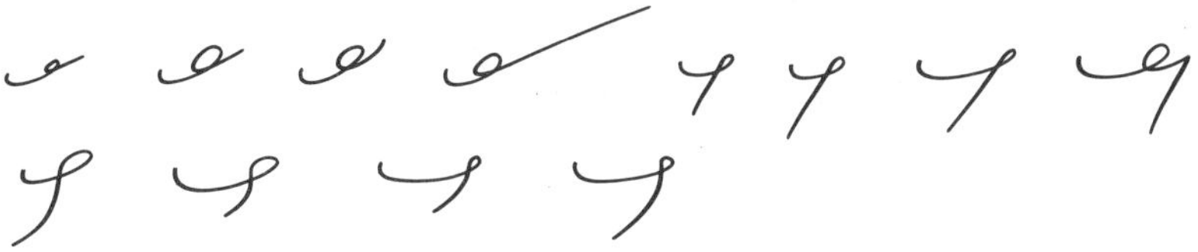

return, rate, rather, rated, reach, ridge, ledge, large, rave, laugh, leaf, live.

PRINCIPLES

Business phrases; *jent-d, pent-d; def-v, tif-v.*

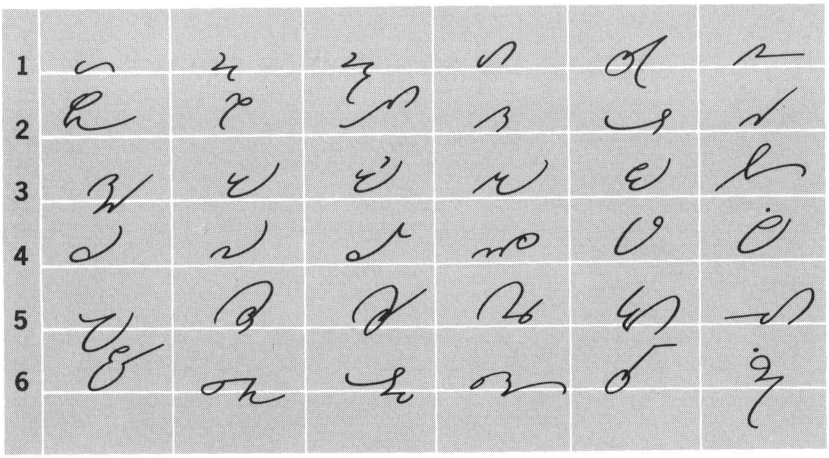

1. of course, as soon as, as soon as possible, of this, I had been, to him.
2. I hope you will, we hope, into this, to us, let us, your order.
3. thank you for your order, was not, wasn't, it was not, he was not, days ago.
4. I want, you want, he wants, worthwhile, gently, happened.
5. regent, devise, divide, definite, positive, motive.
6. expended, I am sure, let us know, weeks ago, I had not, has not been.

BRIEF FORMS AND DERIVATIVES

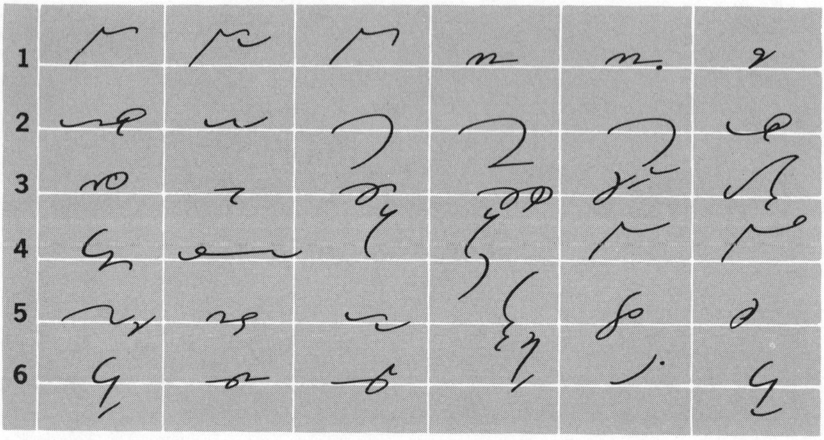

1. direct, director, direction, wonder, wondering, yesterday.
2. recognize, railroad, govern, government, governor, likewise.
3. otherwise, instant-instance, character, characterize, satisfied, automobiles.
4. prosecute, remainder, object, objective, deliver, delivery.
5. greatest, unnecessary, worker, businesses, particularly, side.
6. purchased, anyone, matters, suggested, ending, purchaser.

READING AND SELF-DICTATION PRACTICE

34. Dear Sarah:

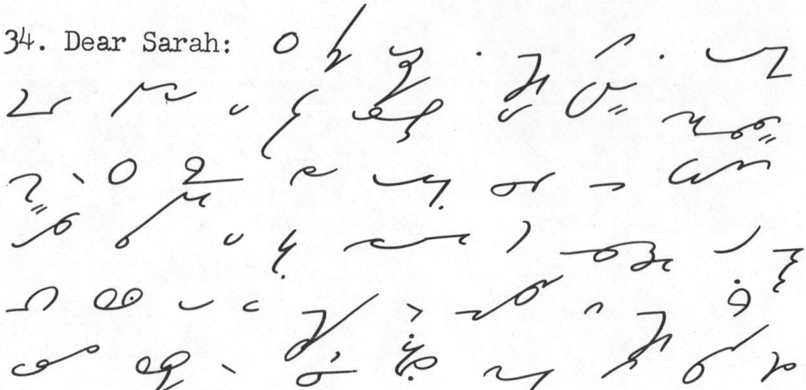

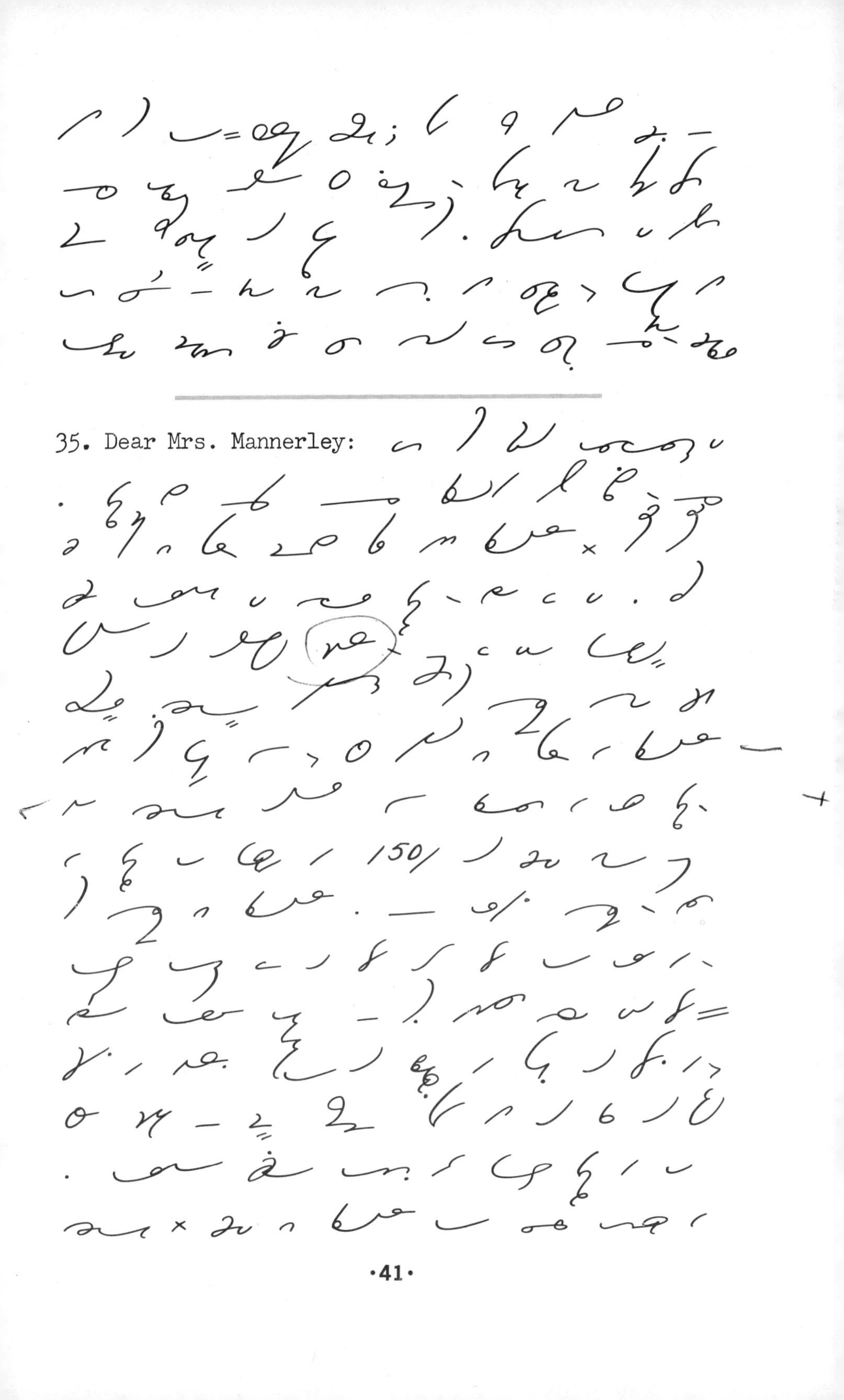

35. Dear Mrs. Mannerley:

150

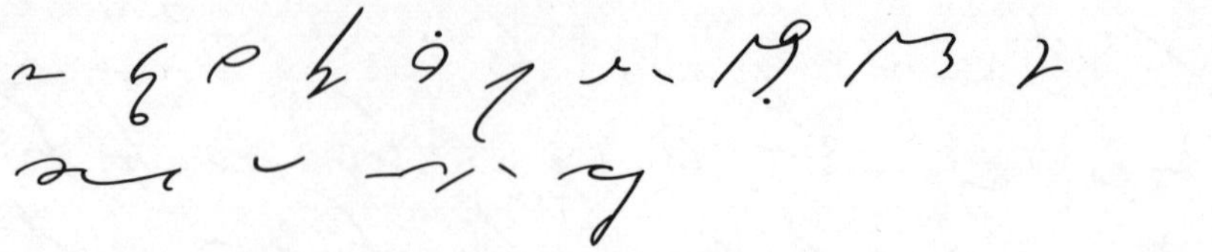

36. Gentlemen: 

37. To the Staff: 

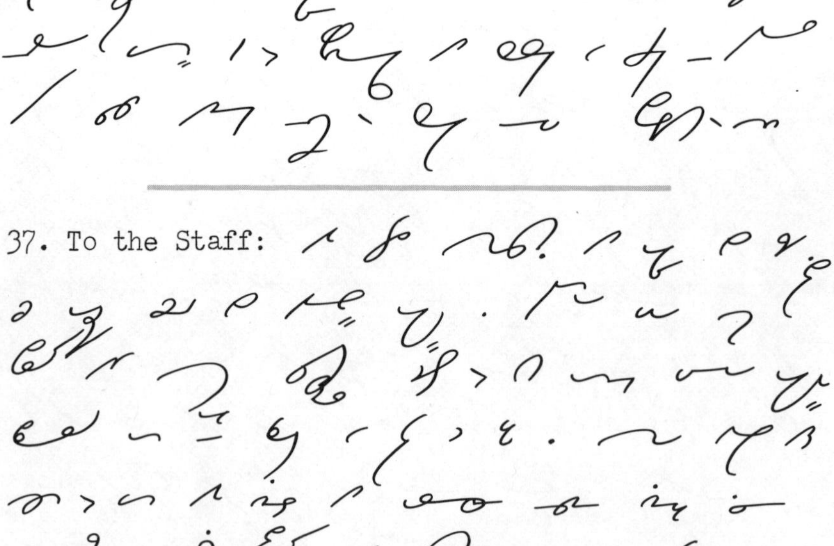

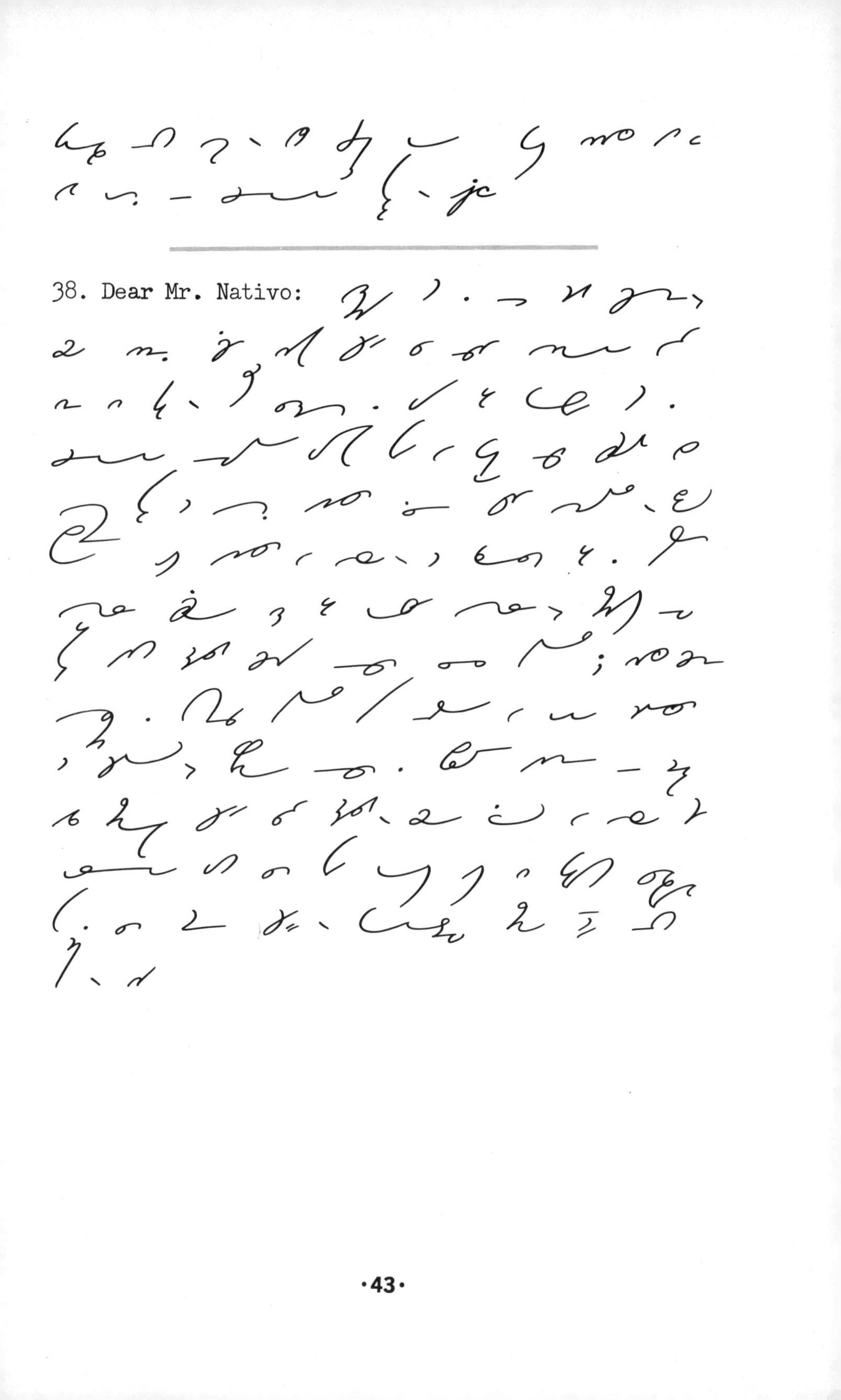

38. Dear Mr. Nativo:

LESSON 10

KNOW YOUR ALPHABET

fr, fer, fk, fek, pr, per, vg, vag, vl, val, bl, bel.

PROPORTION DRILL

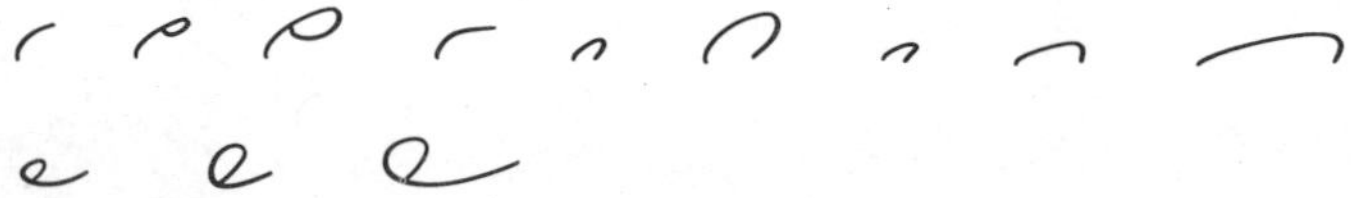

the, they, that, then, you, this, you, can, go, were, where, allow.

PRINCIPLES

Word beginnings *after, al, ul, sub, short-ship, electr-electric;* word endings *cle-cal, self, selves;* intersection.

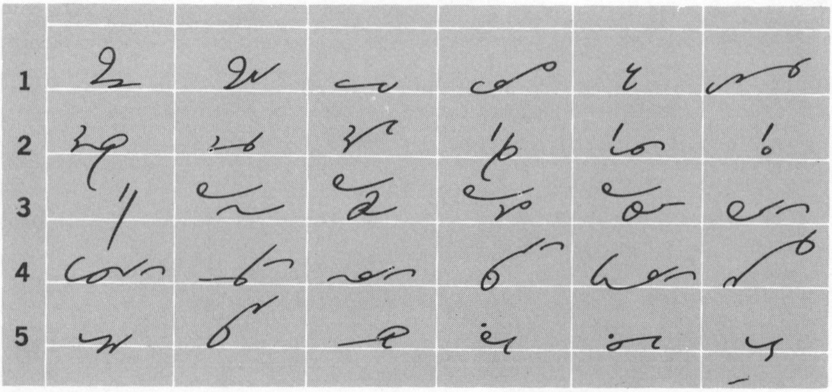

BUT

1. afternoon, afterthought, almost, already, also, altogether.
2. subscribe, submit, substance, shipshape, shipwreck, shortly.
3. shortage, electrical, electric wire, electricity, electric iron, article.
4. practical, medical, critical, identical, political, ultimate.
5. result, adult, myself, herself, himself, ourselves.
6. themselves, a.m., p.m., Chamber of Commerce, C.O.D., Great Britain.
   BUT
7. its, ones, itself, oneself.

BRIEF FORMS AND PHRASES

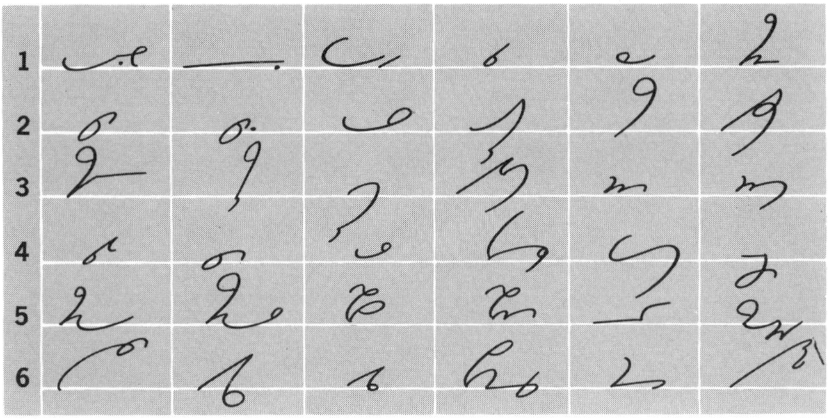

1. willingness, morning, pleased, yet, were, everyone.
2. how-out, outing, like, individuals, advantage, disadvantage.
3. advertisement, agents, covers, discover, success, successful.
4. etc., acknowledge, regard, biggest, progressive, in fact.
5. if you will, I have your letter, we hope that, we hope you can, more than, as a result.
6. to make, would be able, to see, about this matter, from you, to do so.

READING AND SELF-DICTATION PRACTICE

39. Gentlemen: 

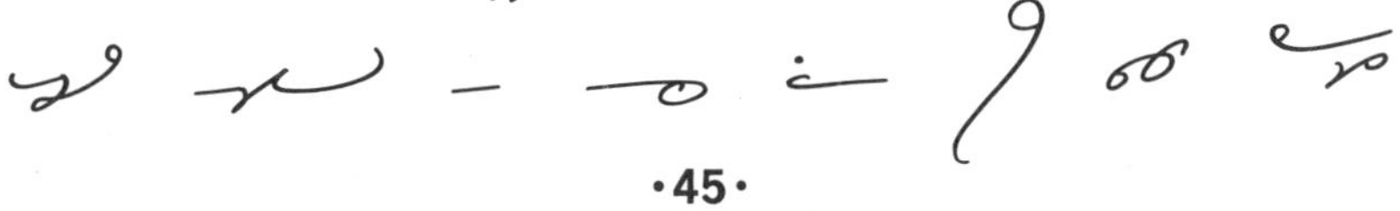

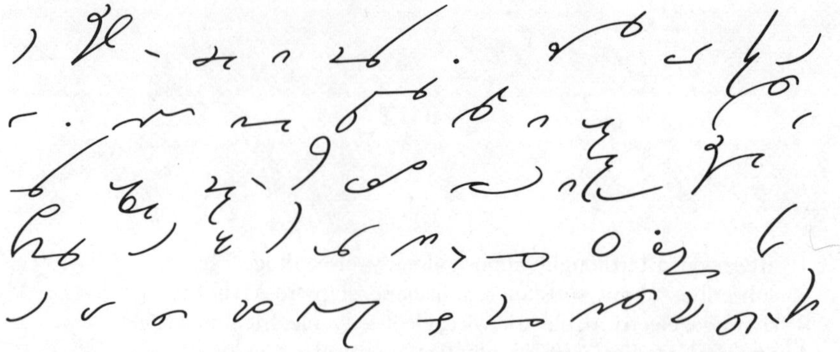

40. Dear John:

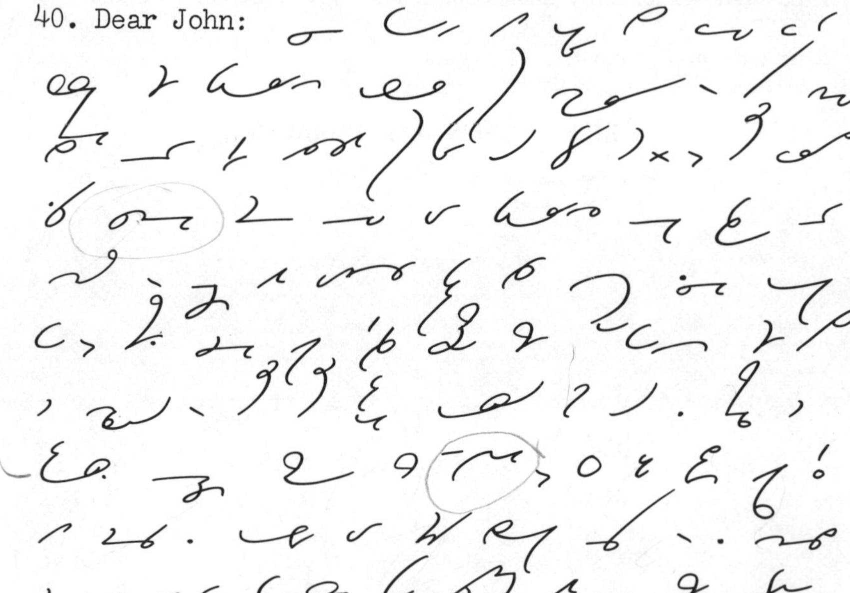

41. Gentlemen:

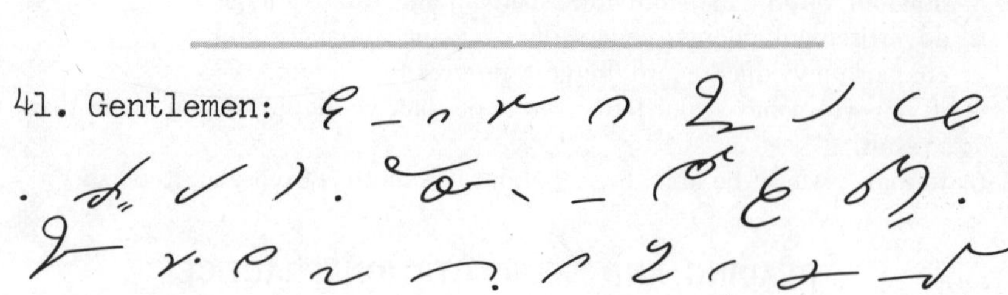

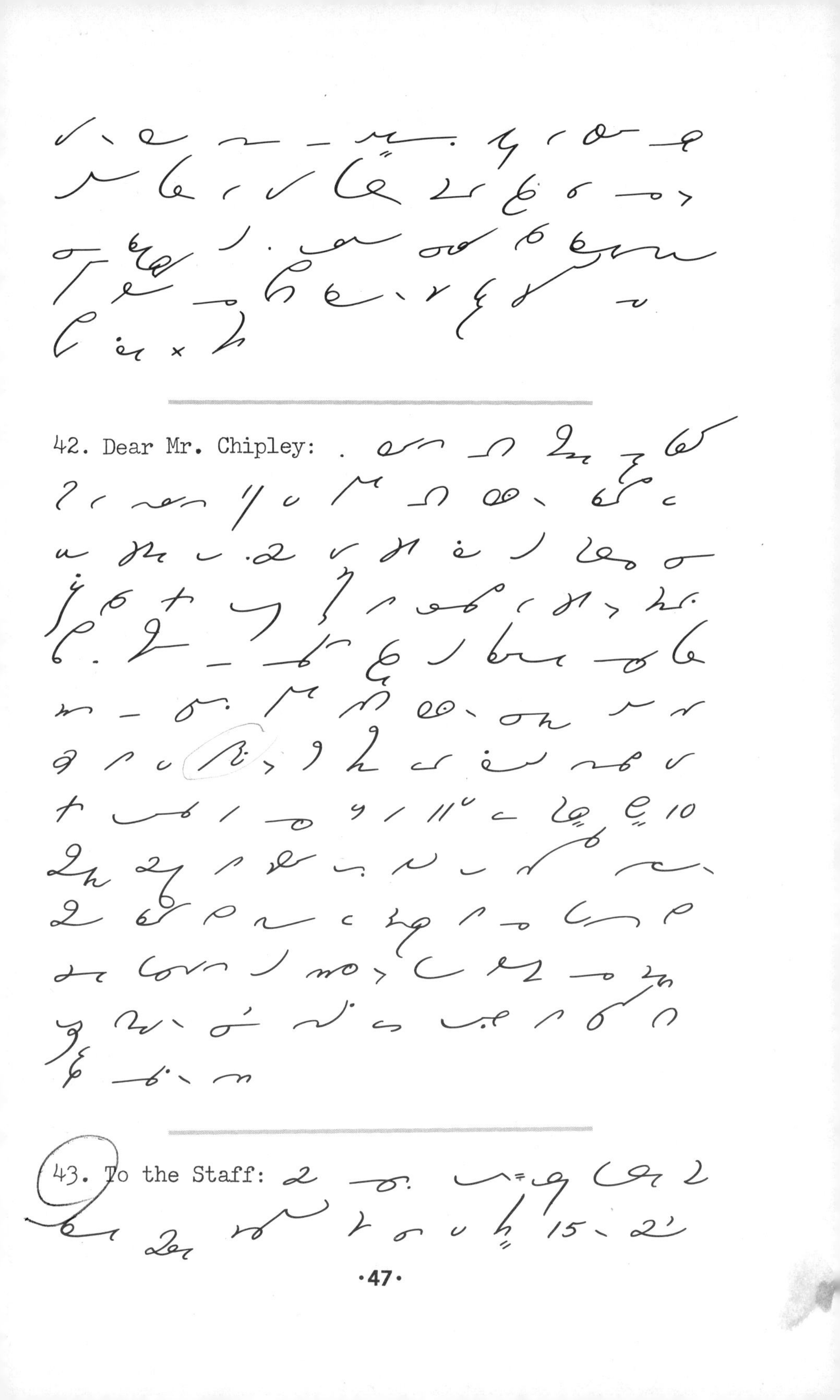

42. Dear Mr. Chipley:

43. To the Staff:

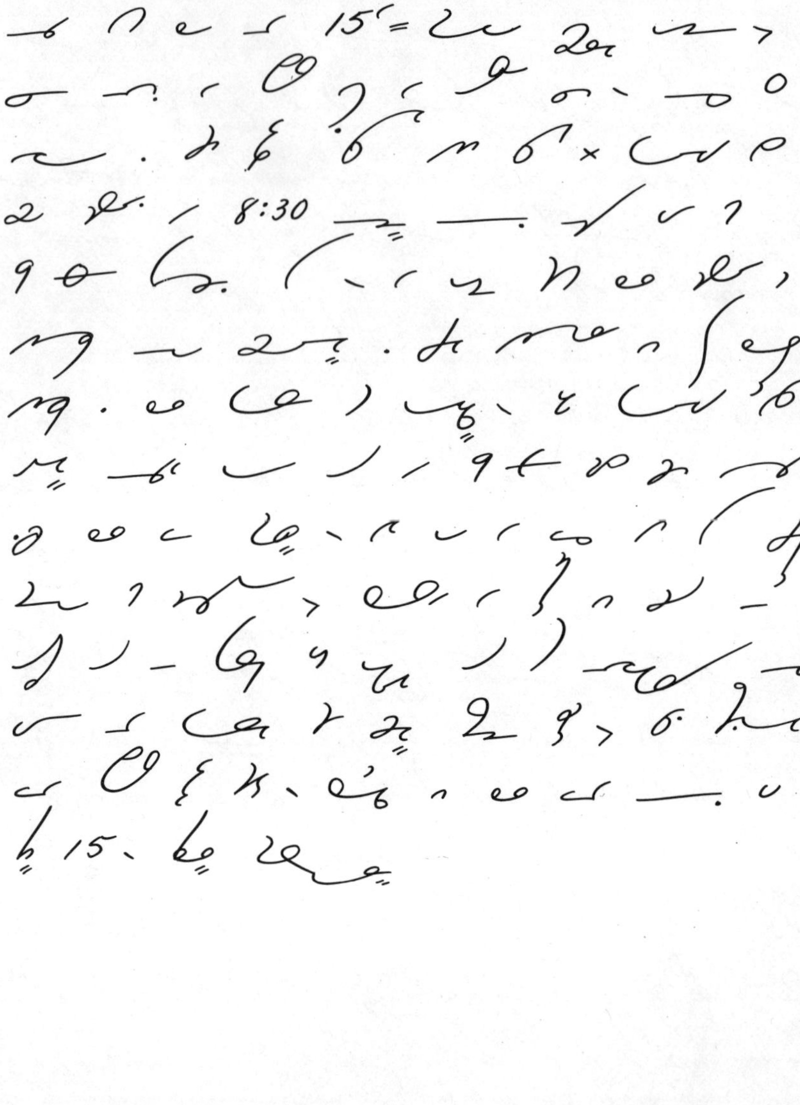

DON'T LET THIS HAPPEN TO YOU!

DICTATED

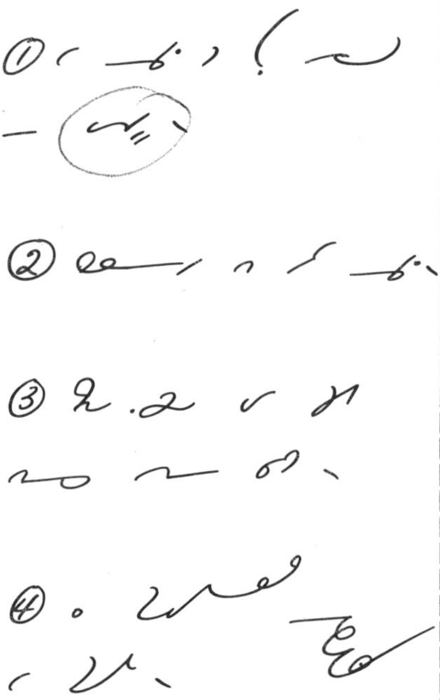

1. The meeting is being called in *October.*

2. I *remembered* you at the meeting.

3. *As* you are aware of the situation, you may come with us.

4. He *fraudulently* misappropriated the funds.

TRANSCRIBED

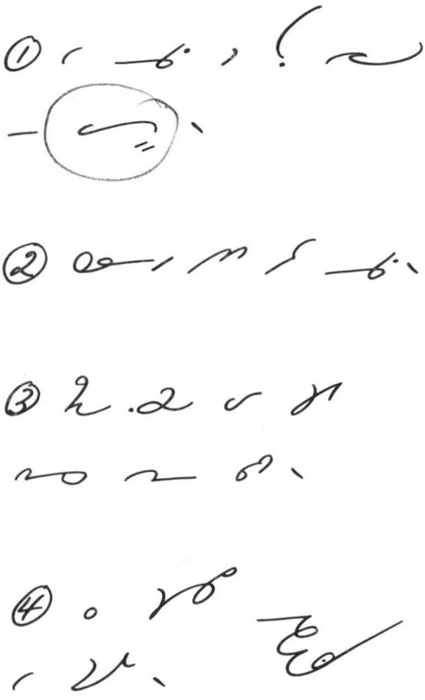

1. The meeting is being called in *August.*

2. I *remitted* to you at the meeting.

3. *If* you are aware of the situation, you may come with us.

4. He *fortunately* misappropriated the funds.

LESSON 11

KNOW YOUR ALPHABET

n, m, ng, nk, p, pent-d, j, jent-d, r, rd, l, ld.

PROPORTION DRILL

as, half, if, advantage, ask, affect, effect, yesterday, effort, after, afford, advertise.

PRINCIPLES

Word beginnings *inter-enter-intro, incl, post, super-supr, trans;* word endings *ship, ful-ify, ification.*

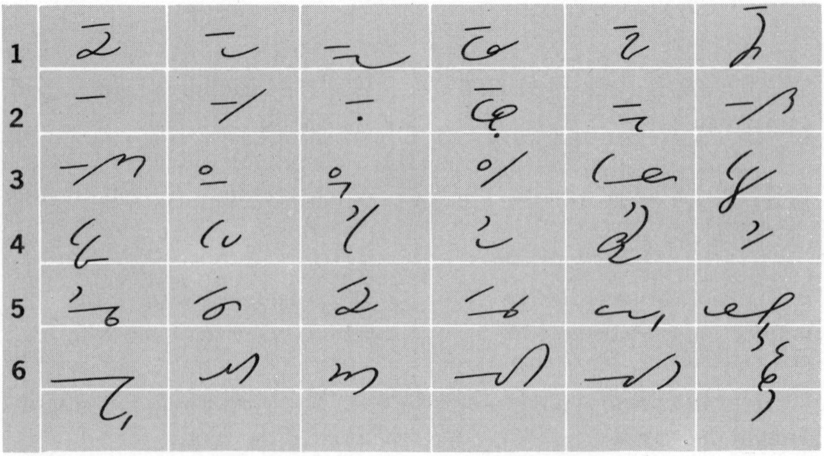

1. interfere, interior, internal, interpret, interrupt, interview.
2. enter, entered, entering, enterprising, entrance, introduce.
3. introduction, incline, inclination, include, postmark, postpaid.
4. postpone, post office, superb, superior, supervisor, support.
5. supremacy, transact, transfer, transmit, ownership, relationships.
6. membership, thoughtful, successful, modify, modification, specification.

FREQUENTLY USED WORDS

Below are 40 of the most frequently used words. (You will notice that you have learned many of them as brief forms.)

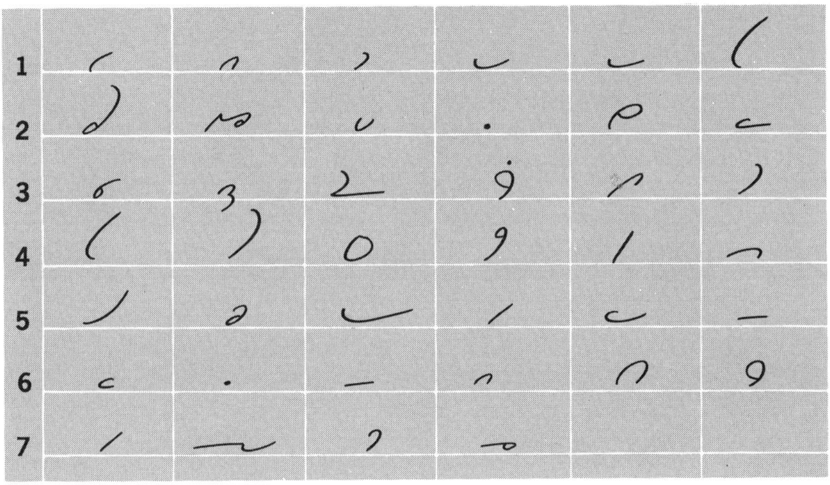

1. the, you, is, are, our, by.
2. very, truly, of, a, that, on.
3. with, yours, from, has, to, for.
4. be, have, I, if, which, can.
5. and, we, will, it, or, not.
6. all, an, in, your, this, as.
7. at, Mr., us, any.

READING AND SELF-DICTATION PRACTICE

44. Dear Mr. Harrold:

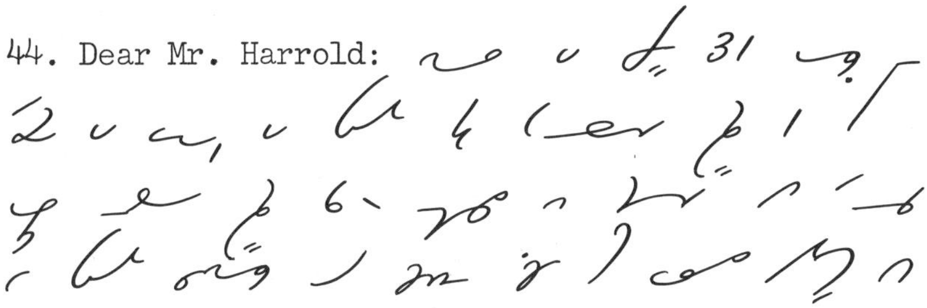

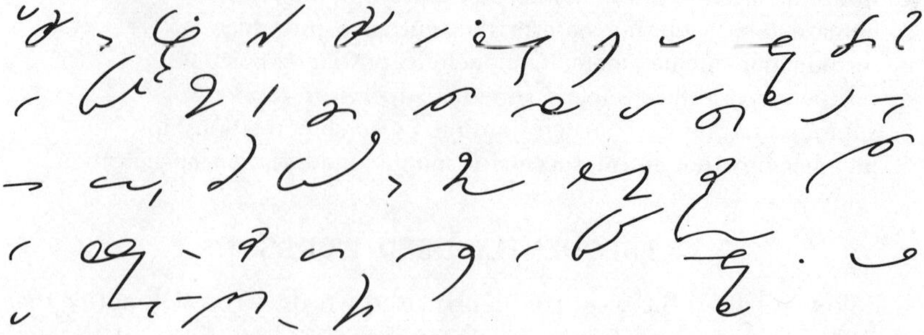

45. Mr. Paragon:

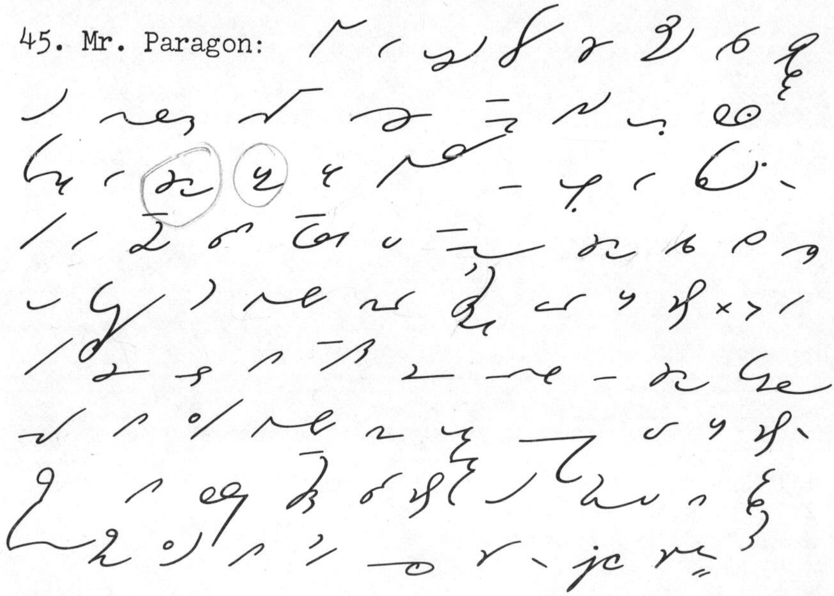

46. Dear Friend:

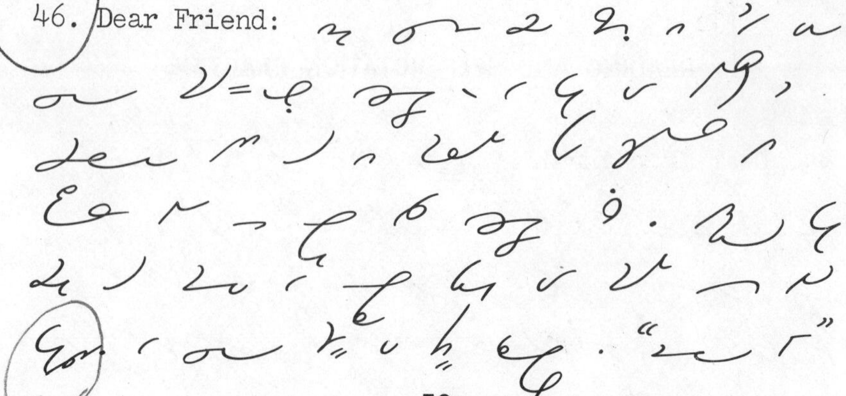

47. Dear Mr. Quincy:

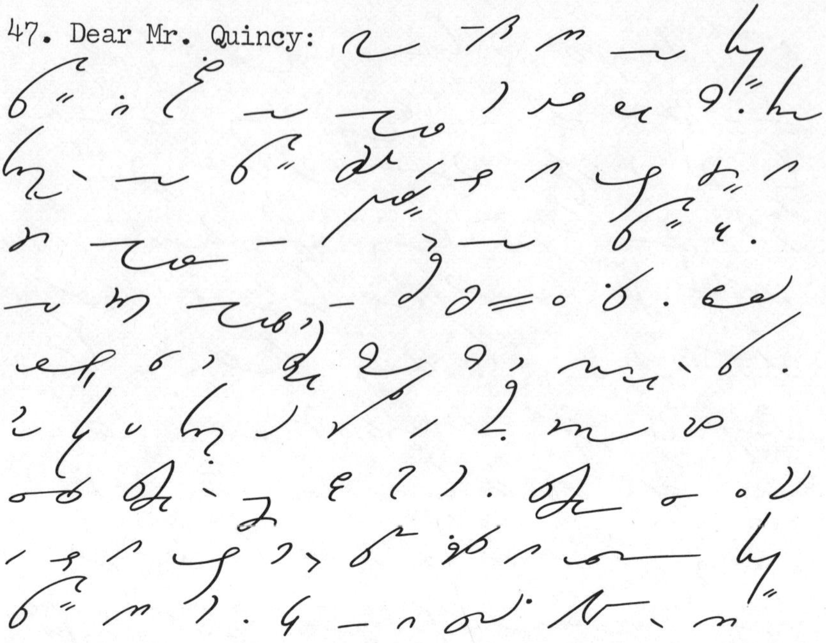

LESSON 12

KNOW YOUR ALPHABET

s, sh, ch, j, s, p, b, pr, pl, br, bl.

PROPORTION DRILL

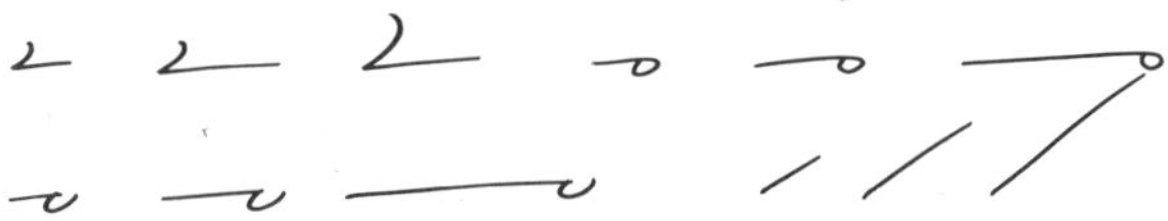

soon, some, from, any, me, many, no, most, memorandum, it, would, did.

PRINCIPLES

Omission of *t, d;* word endings *gram, rity, lity-lty, hood-ward.*

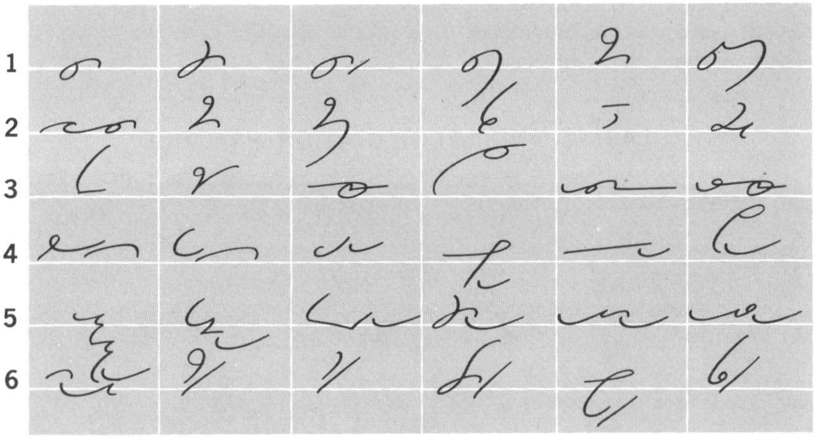

1. act, fact, acted, active, affect, attractive.
2. collect, effect, effective, best, interest, first.
3. bound, extend, mind, demand, recommend, remind.

4. telegram, program, authority, majority, minority, ability.
5. responsibility, personality, punctuality, faculty, locality, loyalty.
6. qualities, afterward, forward, backward, neighborhood, boyhood.

FREQUENTLY USED WORDS

Here are 40 additional words of high frequency.

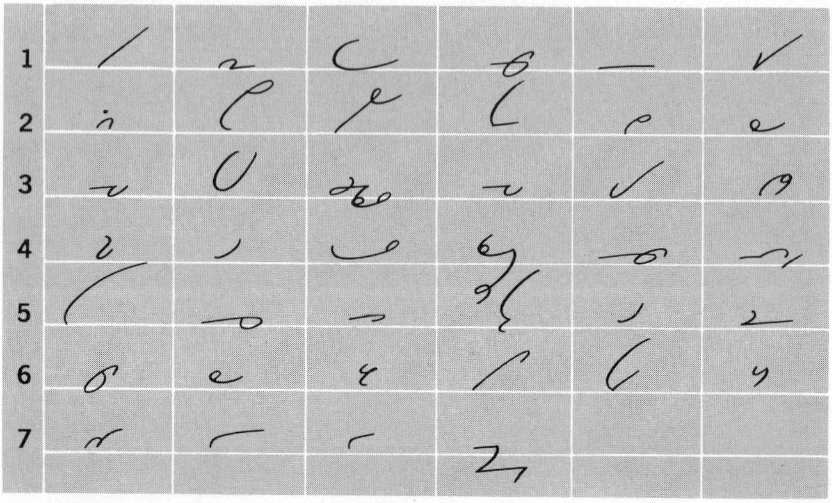

1. would, one, please, now, more, should.
2. who, about, dear, been, they, year.
3. no, gentlemen, sincerely, know, order, these.
4. so, there, letter, service, make, enclosed.
5. time, may, new, business, their, some.
6. out, were, was, do, but, office.
7. other, them, than, information.

READING AND SELF-DICTATION PRACTICE

48. Dear Mr. Marris:

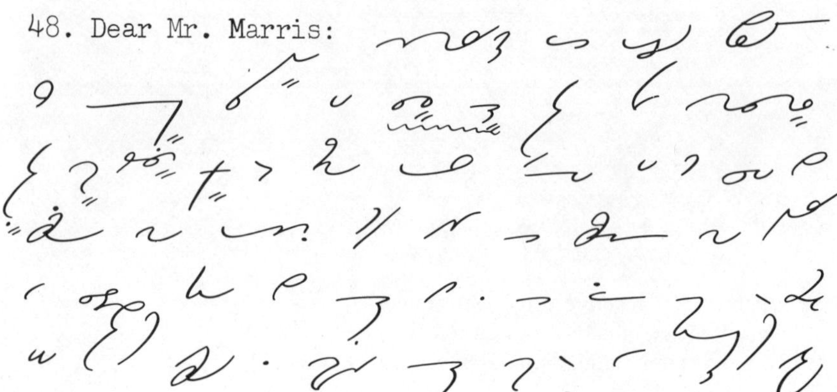

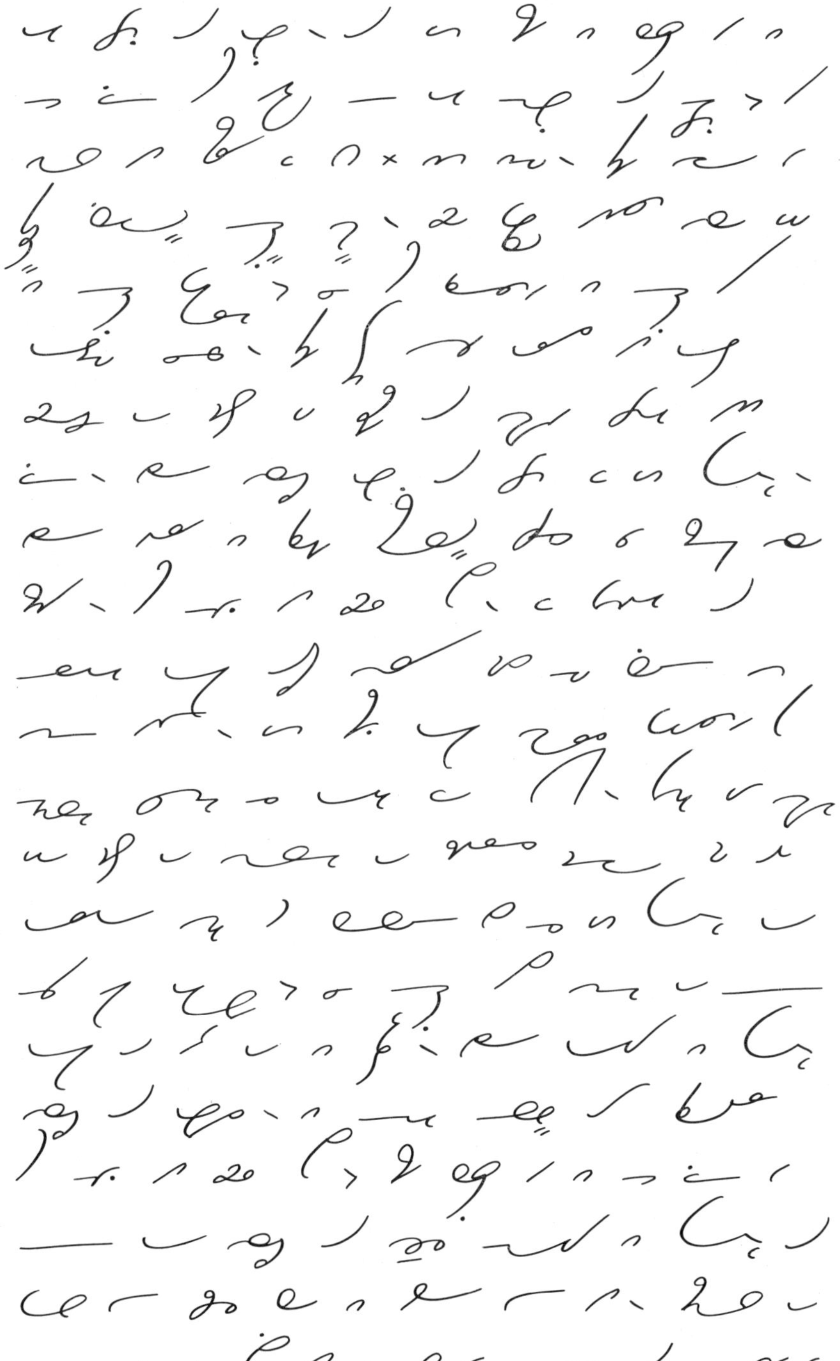

49. Dear Mrs. Beach:

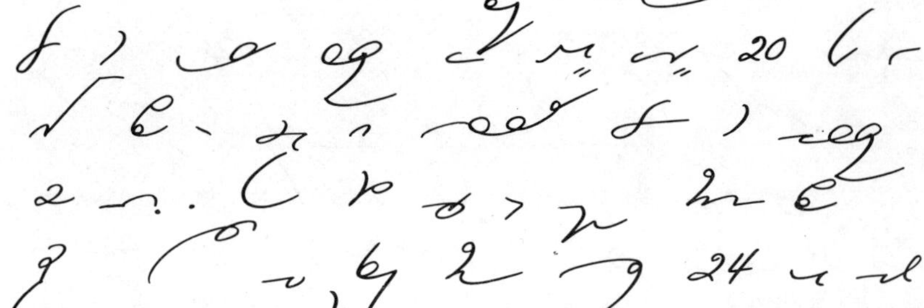

50. Dear Fred:

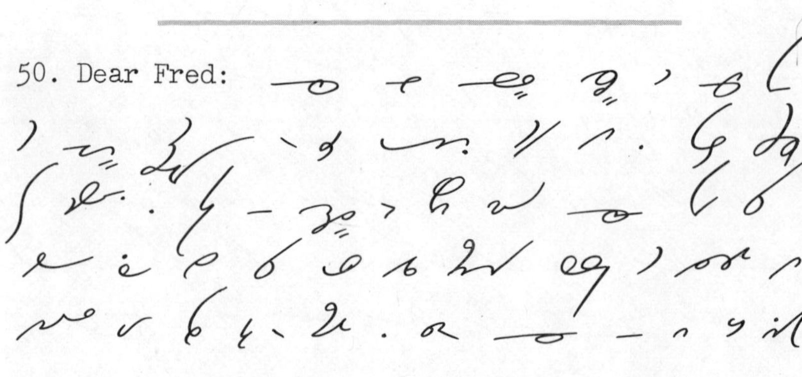

51. Dear Mr. Jeffrey:

52. Dear Miss Wolf:

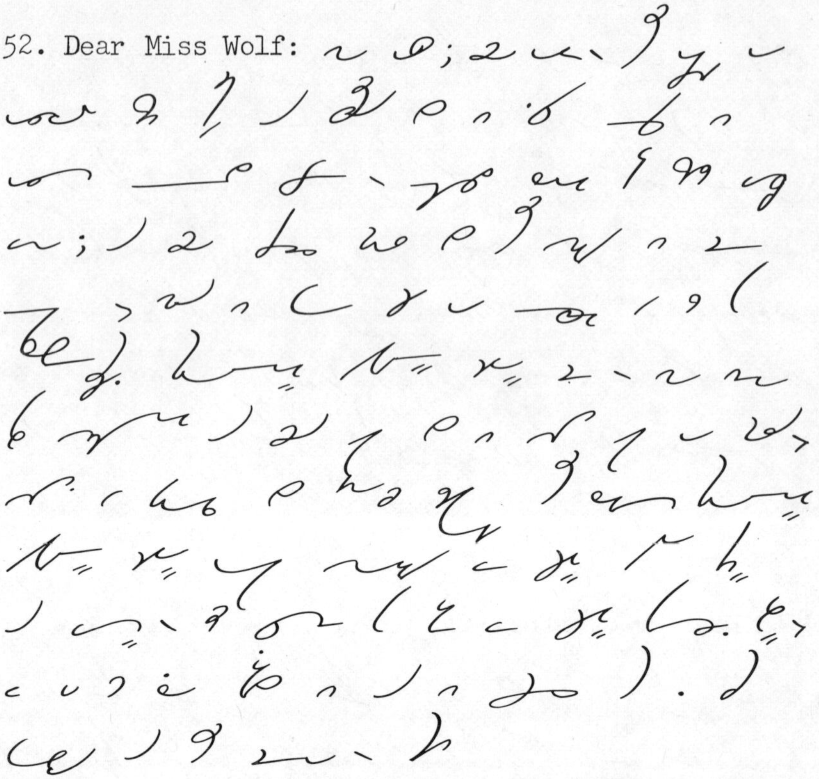

LESSON 13

KNOW YOUR ALPHABET

n, m, th, nt, mt, th, ten, tem, r, rd, l, ld.

PROPORTION DRILL

you, use, he can, I, how, I can, own, home, whole, core, call, goal.

PRINCIPLES

Word beginnings *self-circum, under;* word endings *sume, sumption, ulate;* proper name terminations.

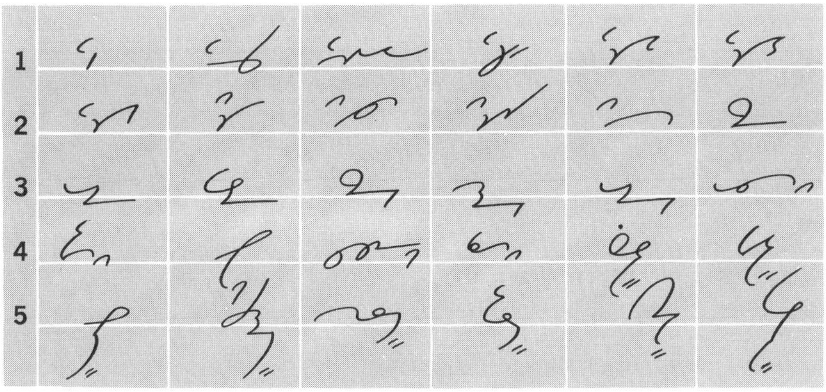

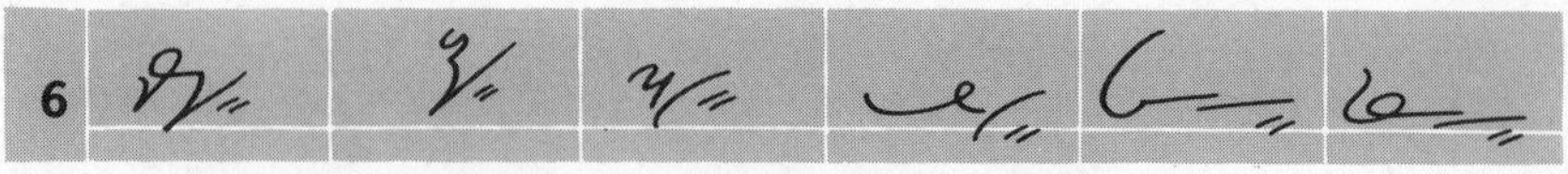

BUT

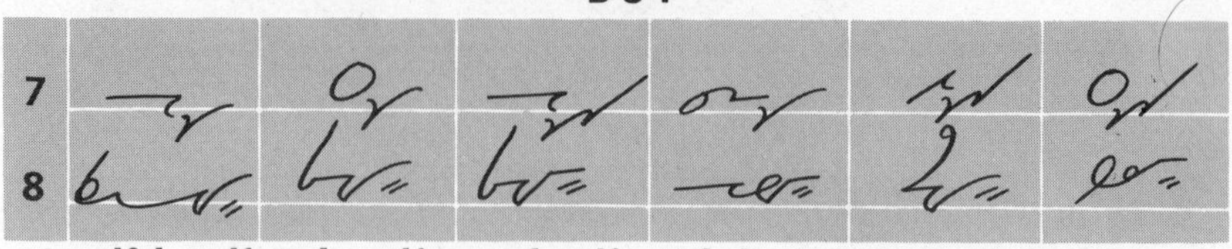

1. selfish, self-made, self-control, self-satisfied, circumstance, circumstances.
2. circumstantial, understand, undertake, understood, undergo, assume.
3. resume, presume, assumption, consumption, resumption, regulate.
4. speculate, tabulation, accumulation, circulate, Harrisburg, Pittsburgh.
5. Nashville, Jacksonville, Greenfield, Springfield, Davenport, Bridgeport.
6. Stanford, Oxford, Washington, Lexington, Birmingham, Framingham.

BUT

7. misunderstand, I understand, misunderstood, I cannot understand, it is understood, I understood.
8. Charleston, Johnston, Johnstown, Morristown, Evanston, Tarrytown.

FREQUENTLY USED WORDS

Here are 40 more words of high frequency.

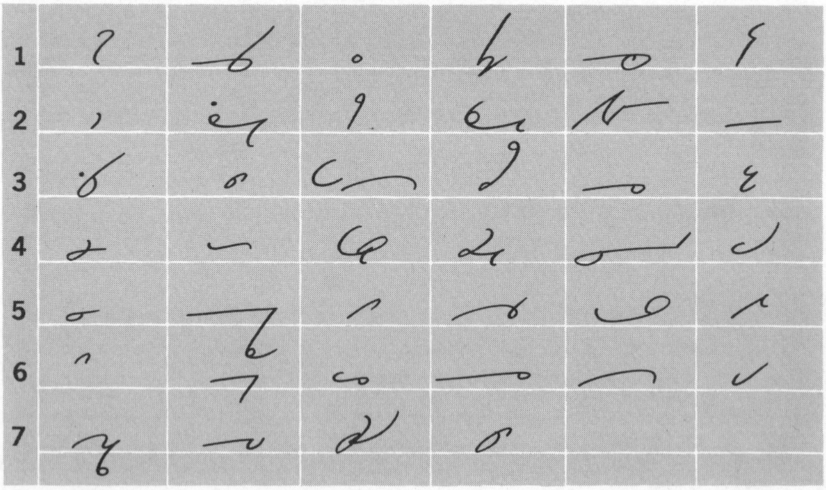

1. up, made, he, just, my, such.
2. his, help, each, sales, department, am.
3. had, use, program, every, me, also.
4. send, work, price, first, amount, want.
5. when, manager, two, get, like, its.
6. under, much, only, many, good, what.
7. copy, most, find, how.

53. Dear Mr. Johnston: 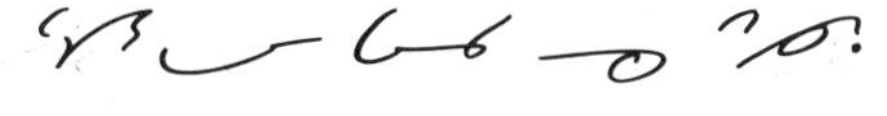

54. Gentlemen: 

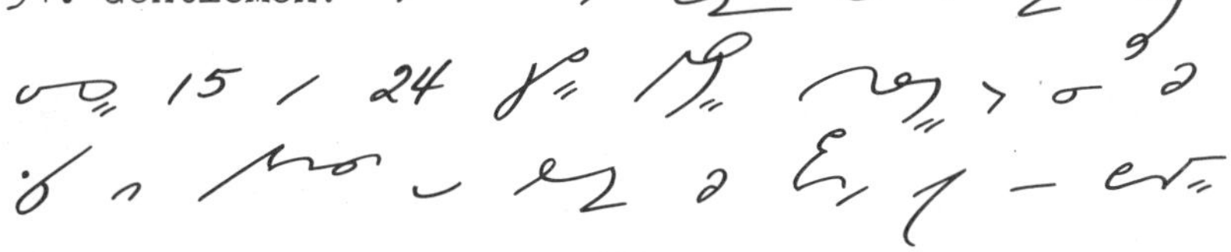

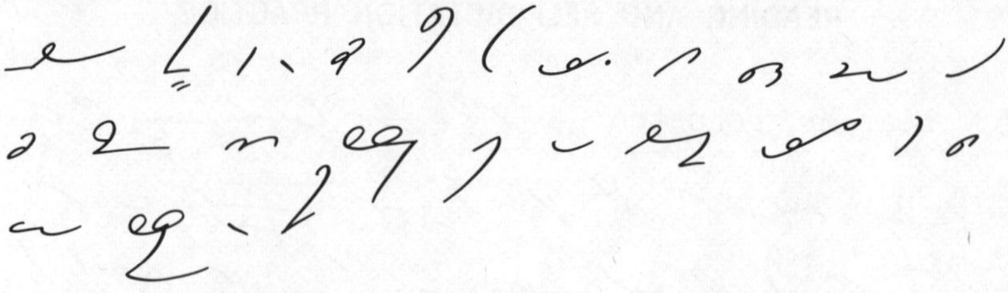

55. Dear Mr. Hart: 

56. Dear Customer: 

LESSON 14

KNOW YOUR ALPHABET

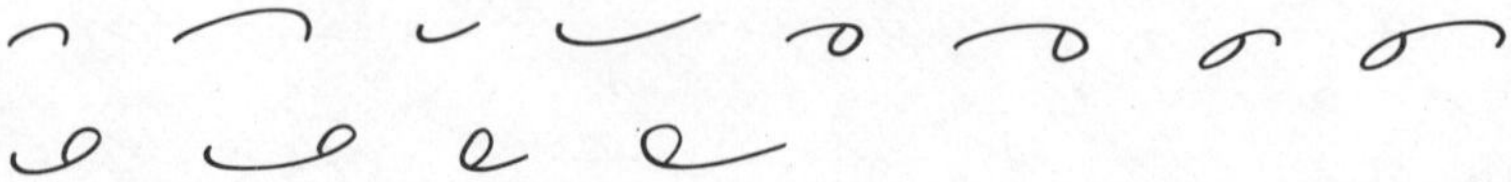

k, g, r, l, ka, ga, ak, ag, ra, la, ar, al.

PROPORTION DRILL

keys, guess, case, gaze, rest, less, next, miss, teas, days, fees, face.

PRINCIPLES

Abbreviations – word families: *use, titude, titute, cate, gate, quire, ntic, ology, tribute, quent, itis, iety.*

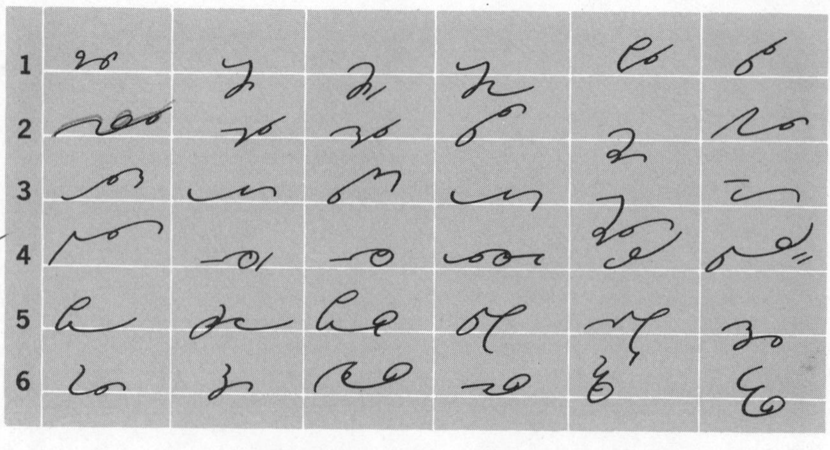

1. excuse, refuse, confused, refusal, aptitude, attitude.
2. gratitude, institute, constitute, adequate, confiscate, duplicate.
3. indicates, locate, education, location, investigate, interrogate.
4. delegate, inquired, inquiry, requirements, authentic, Atlantic.
5. apology, psychology, apologize, attribute, contribution, consequently.
6. frequent, subsequent, tonsillitis, neuritis, society, propriety.

FREQUENTLY USED WORDS

Here are 40 additional words of high frequency.

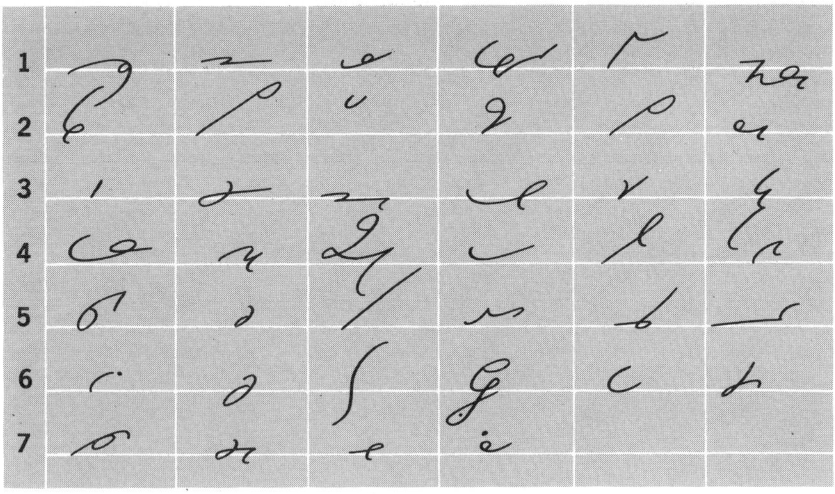

1. give, number, return, president, during, insurance.
2. best, today, over, after, day, years.
3. shall, same, numbers, last, state, possible.
4. plan, cost, available, well, days, those.
5. attention, see, date, through, need, month.
6. thank, way, before, appreciate, per, check.
7. take, since, next, here.

READING AND SELF-DICTATION PRACTICE

57. Mr. Guest: 

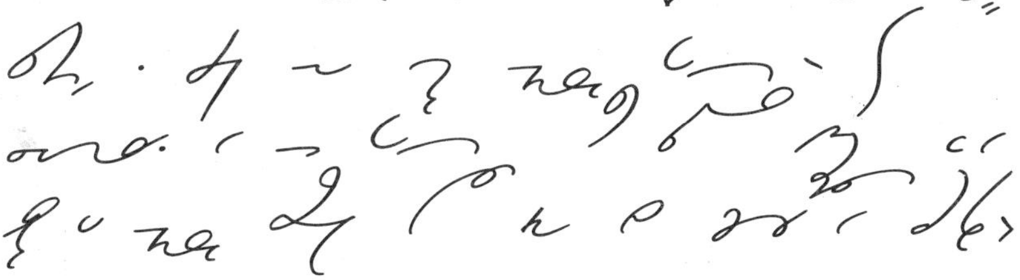

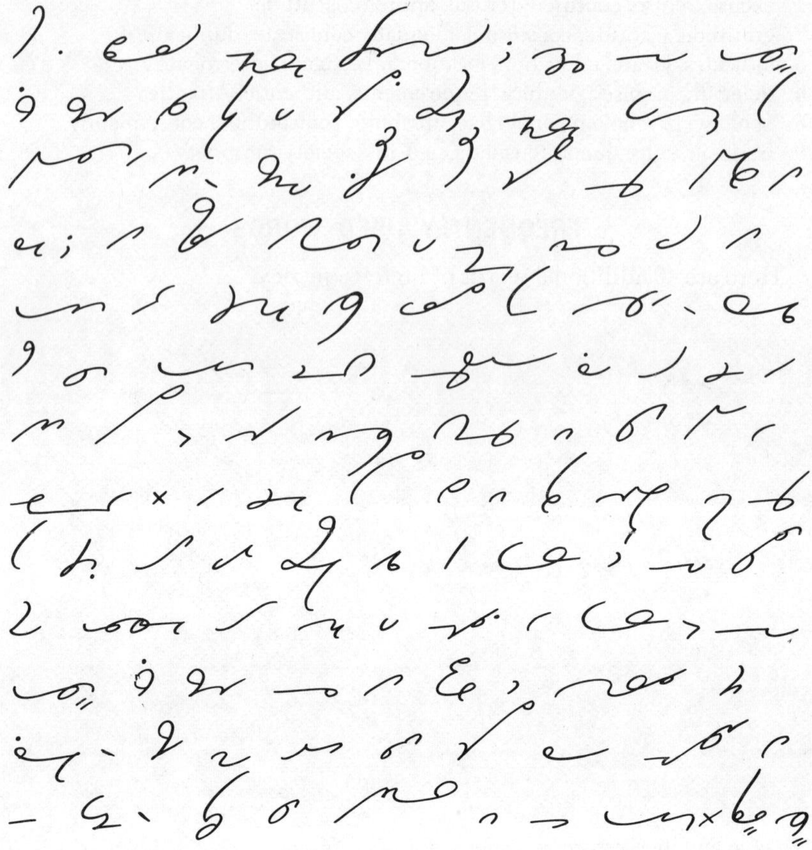

58. Dear Mrs. Nestor:

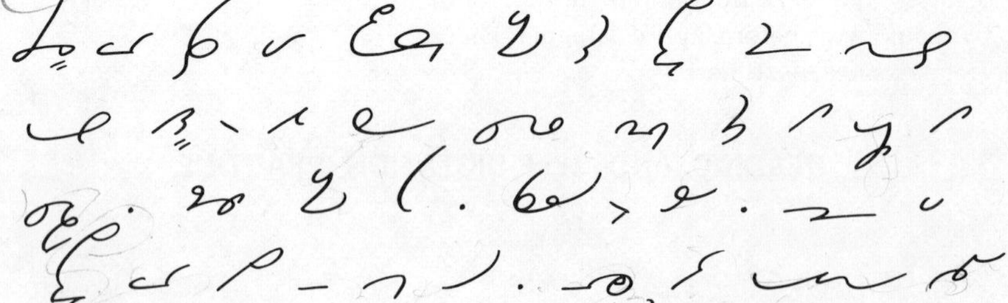

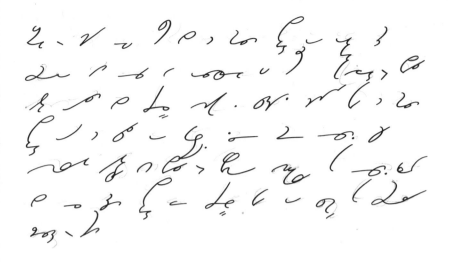

59. Dear Doctor Fisher:

60. Dear Mr. Collins:

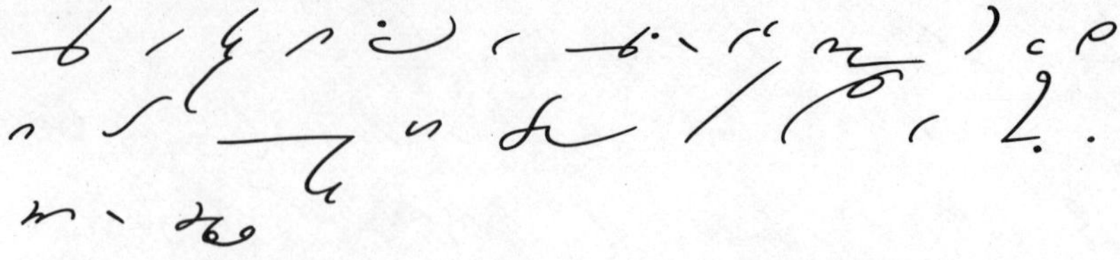

61. Dear Mrs. Gardiner: 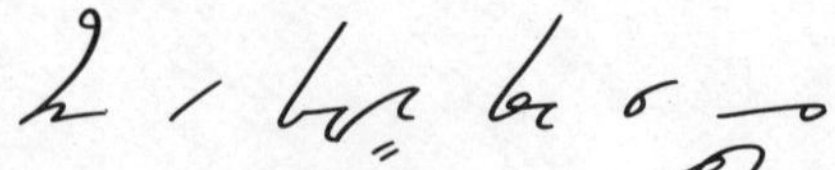

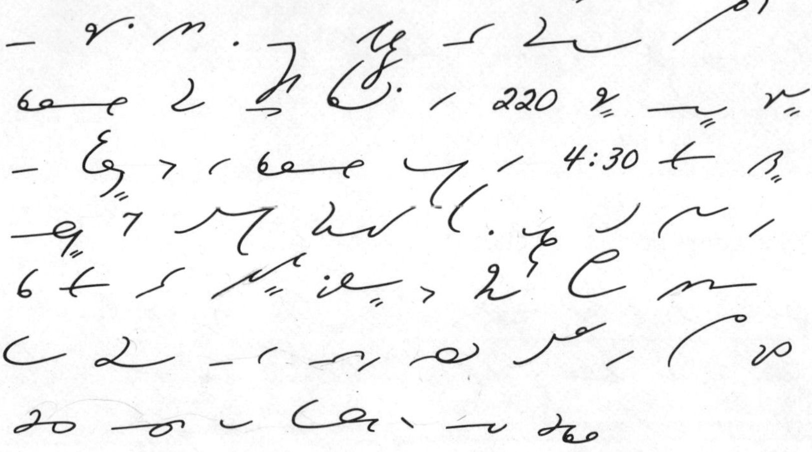

LESSON 15

KNOW YOUR ALPHABET

sks, sgs, sns, sms, sts.

PROPORTION DRILL

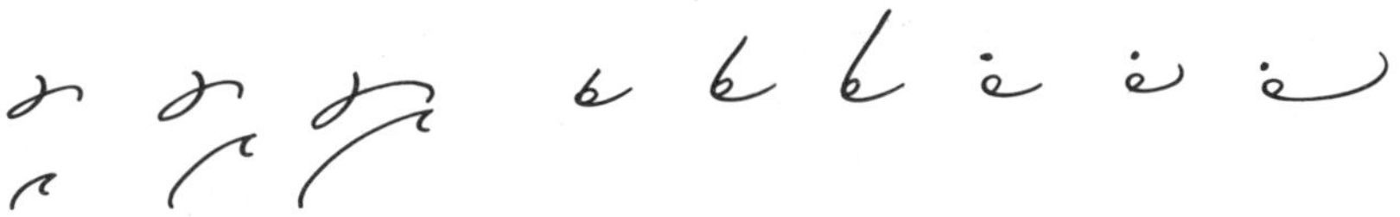

seek, sake, sag, sheer, cheer, jeer, here, heard, held, those, tense, times.

PRINCIPLES

Abbreviations – not in families; omission of words in phrases; common geographical abbreviations.

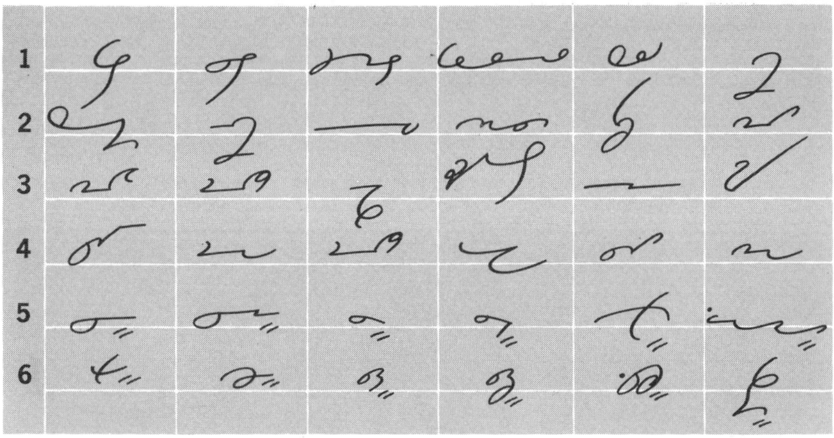

1. privilege, anniversary, significant, preliminary, arithmetic, convenient.
2. alphabetic, inconvenient, memorandum, curriculum, by the way, one or two.
3. one of those, some of these, in the past, we should like to have, more and more, up to date.

4. out of town, some of our, some of these, will you please, week or two, one of our.
5. America, American, England, English, Great Britain, Honolulu.
6. Puerto Rico, Canada, U. S., U. S. A., Hawaii, Pacific.

FREQUENTLY USED WORDS

Here are 40 additional words of high frequency.

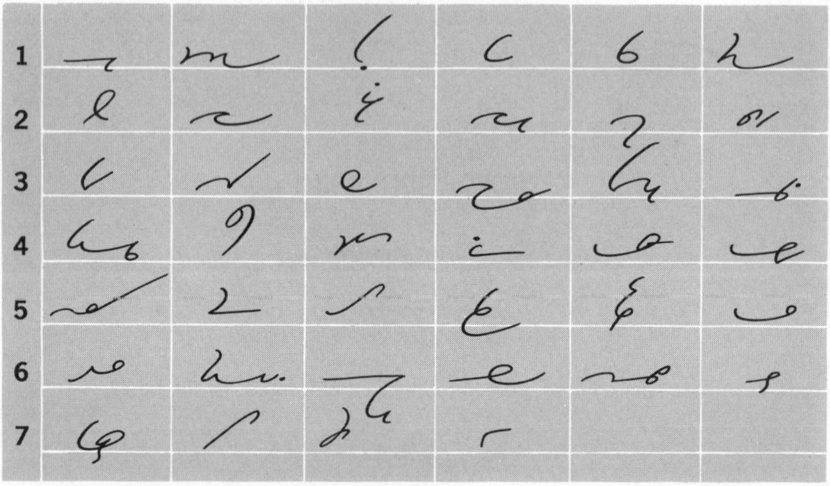

1. must, school, being, present, pay, full.
2. tax, call, hope, course, company, used.
3. part, could, where, complete, because, meeting.
4. policy, however, stock, home, line, list.
5. credit, form, into, people, special, let.
6. three, following, members, mail, committee, necessary.
7. prices, do, few, then.

READING AND SELF-DICTATION PRACTICE

62. Dear Mrs. Held:

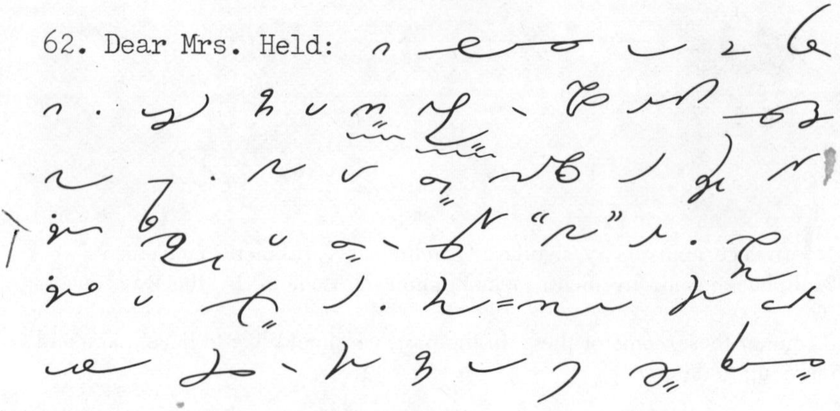

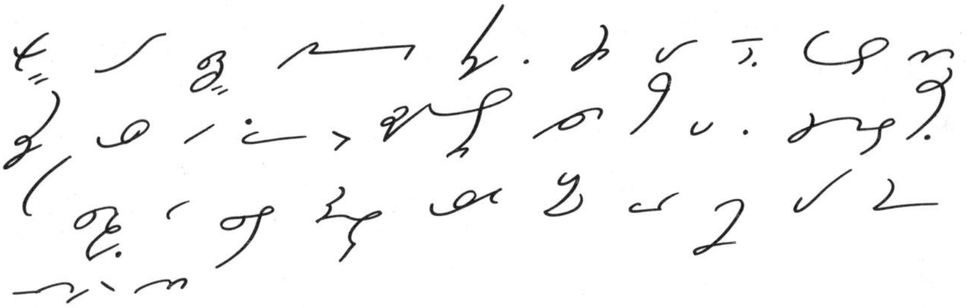

63. Dear Carol: 

64. ARE YOU EFFICIENT OR DO YOU JUST GET BY?

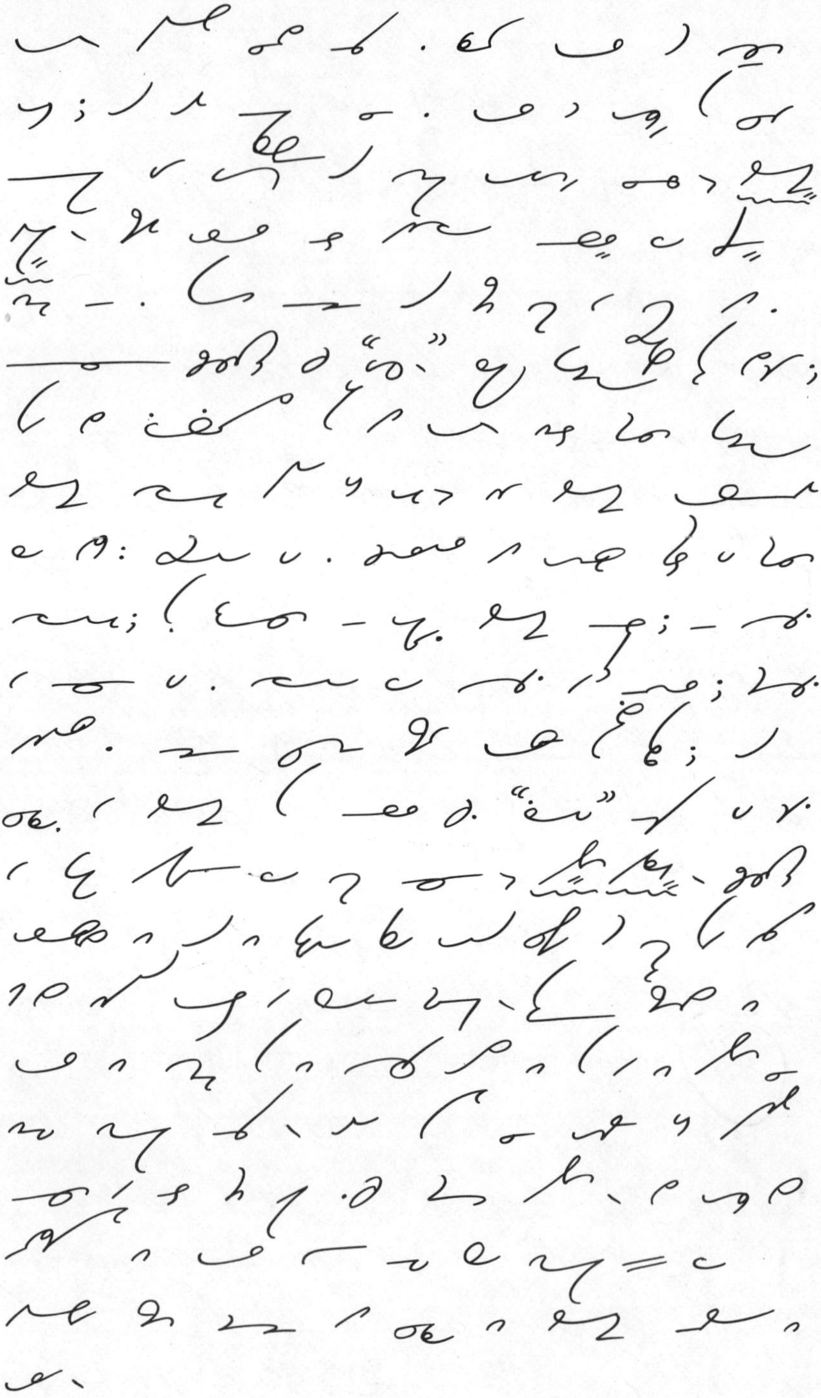

DON'T LET THIS HAPPEN TO YOU!

DICTATED

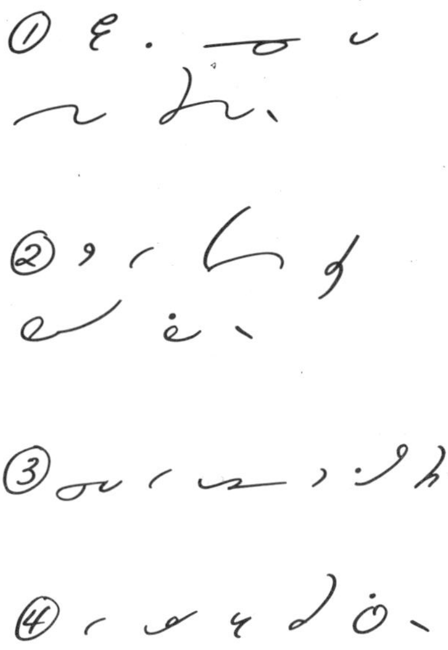

1. He was a man of great *vigor.*

2. He is the big *chief* around here.

3. I know the room is *handy* for you.

4. The *return* was very high.

TRANSCRIBED

1. He was a man of great *fig-ure.*

2. He is the big *cheese* around here.

3. I know the room is *empty* for you.

4. The *rate* was very high.

LESSON 16

PRINCIPLES

Lessons 16 through 20 include another type of review. The first letter or article of Lessons 16-20 will emphasize brief forms and words of high frequency; the remainder of the Reading and Self-Dictation Practice exercises will review the principles. The following chart includes all the vowels and vowel joinings.

1. mailing, favor, own, cushion, piano, noise.
2. equipment, folio, deeds, free, know, stood.
3. area, annoyance, quota, poems, carriage, bank.
4. lower, production, creation, doubt, twice, drawee.
5. tiny, little, law, wages, dial, proud.
6. square, radio, practice, replenished, solved, worry.
7. prior, railway, bureau, appliance, greedy, seller.
8. whole, worst, appreciate, reviews, yes, via.
9. seats, healthy, call, swift, bias, unite.
10. youth, association, days, charming, move, switch.
11. ahead, power, yarn, variation, acting, hurry.
12. formula, while, aware, dispute, yellow, initiate.
13. prices, firm, precious, wheat, away, now.
14. Yale, rayon.

FREQUENTLY USED WORDS

Here are 40 additional words of high frequency.

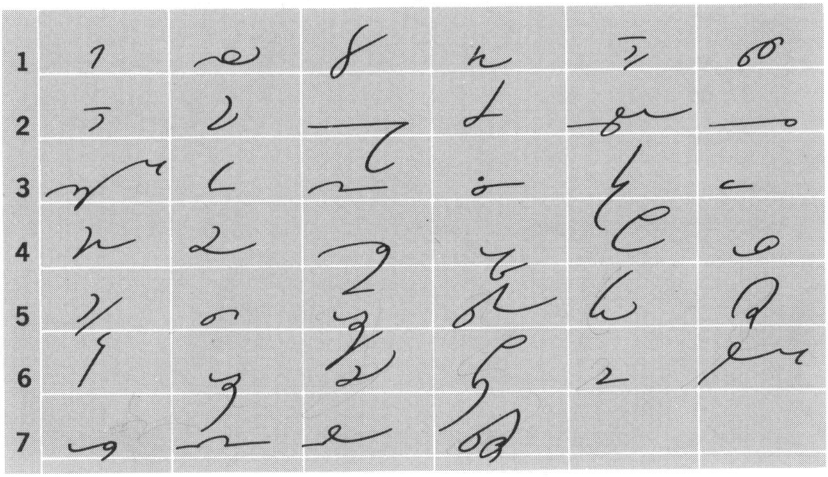

1. wish, card, paid, sure, interested, without.
2. interest, further, member, general, material, money.
3. customers, upon, come, him, job, own.
4. future, feel, given, report, able, write.
5. forward, week, received, additional, board, division.
6. subject, receive, sent, above, soon, dealers.
7. request, income, until, advise.

READING AND SELF-DICTATION PRACTICE

65. Dear Mrs. Strong: 

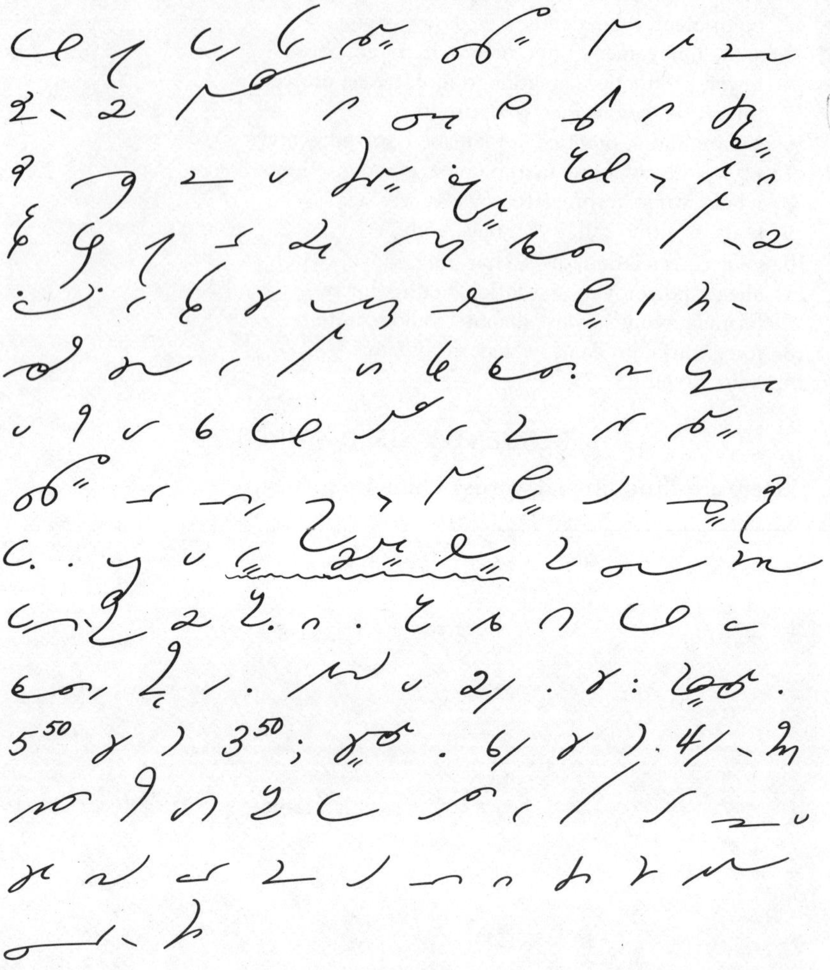

66. Dear Mr. Yale:

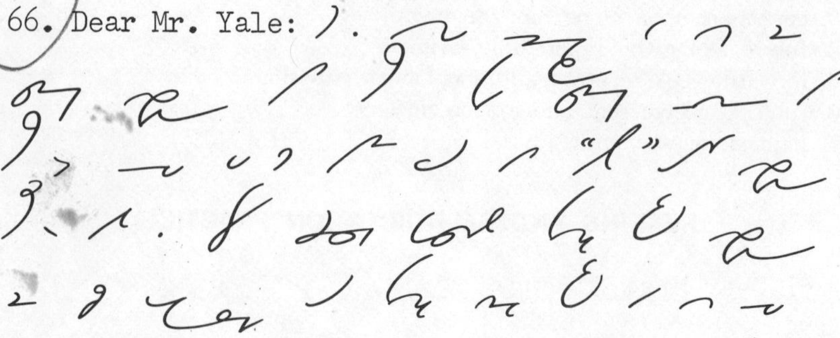

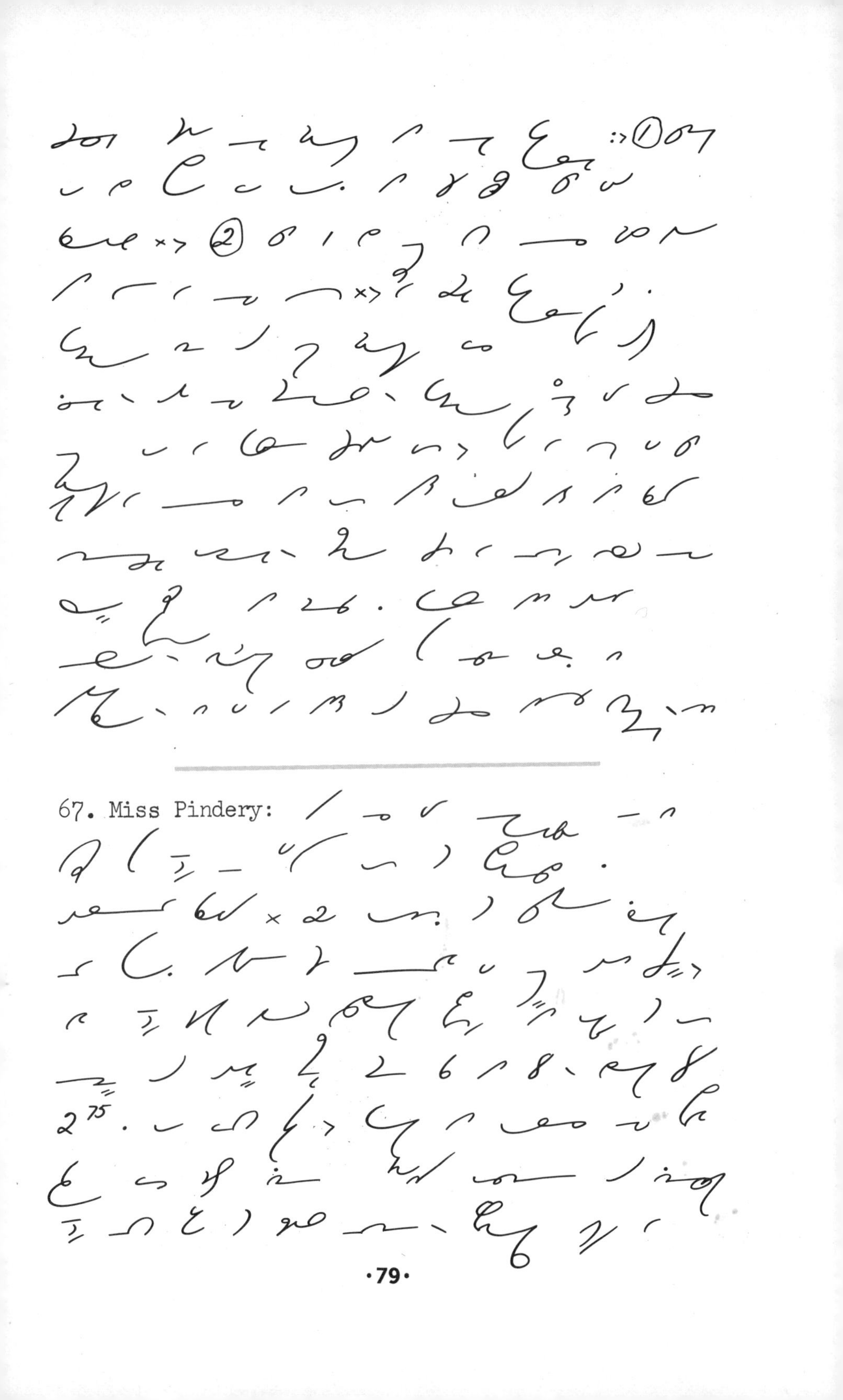

67. Miss Pindery:

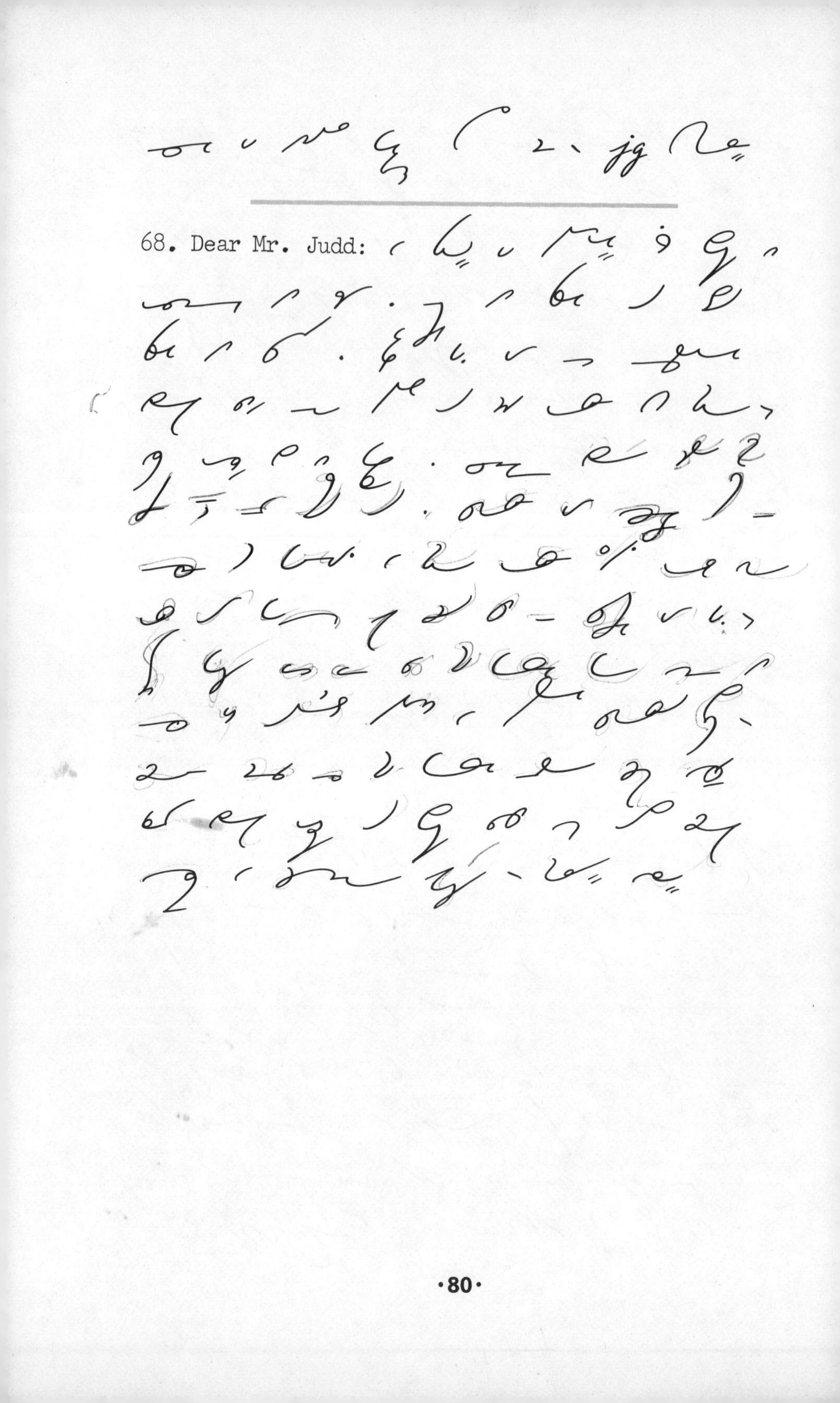

68. Dear Mr. Judd:

LESSON 17

PRINCIPLES

The following chart contains all the *joined* word beginnings.

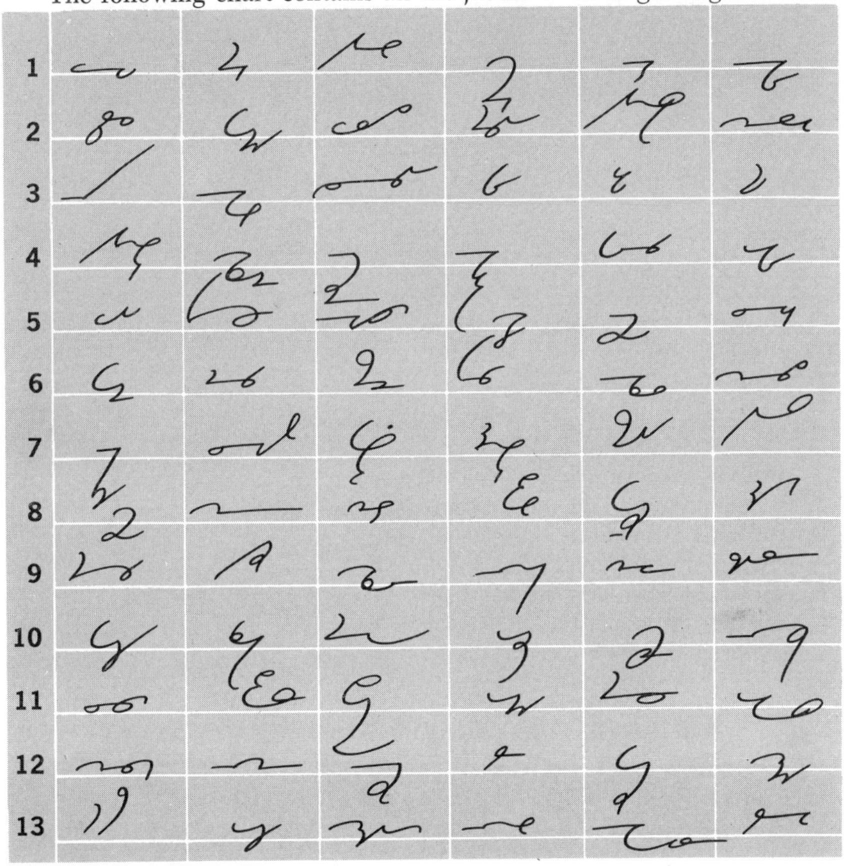

1. almost, furnish, dismiss, convention, insist, import.
2. attorney, pursuit, already, furniture, describe, commerce.
3. indeed, impression, thermometer, port, also, further.
4. description, comparison, investment, impossible, permit, report.
5. although, began, mistake, compete, unfair, emotion.
6. person, submit, afternoon, beneath, misery, committee.
7. unjust, immodest, perhaps, subscription, afterthought, delay.
8. confer, common, unnecessary, express, persuasion, substantial.
9. forget, decision, concern, encourage, unknown, extreme.

10. proceed, suburb, formal, receive, confine, engage.
11. enact, explain, approval, result, foreman, reply.
12. connection, income, emphasis, turn, provision, consult.
13. forever, receipt, construct, increase, employment, terms.

FREQUENTLY USED WORDS

Here are 40 additional words of high frequency.

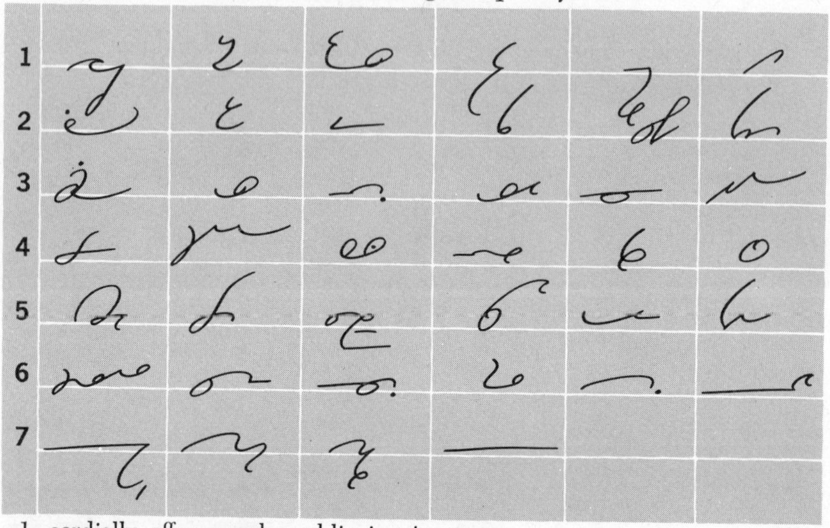

1. cordially, offer, supply, public, invoice, too.
2. held, opportunity, shipment, believe, attached, book.
3. while, right, enclosing, rates, name, total.
4. payment, federal, area, increase, past, why.
5. defense, back, equipment, items, loan, better.
6. secretary, again, making, free, going, months.
7. membership, group, copies, men.

READING AND SELF-DICTATION PRACTICE

69. Dear Mr. Johnson:

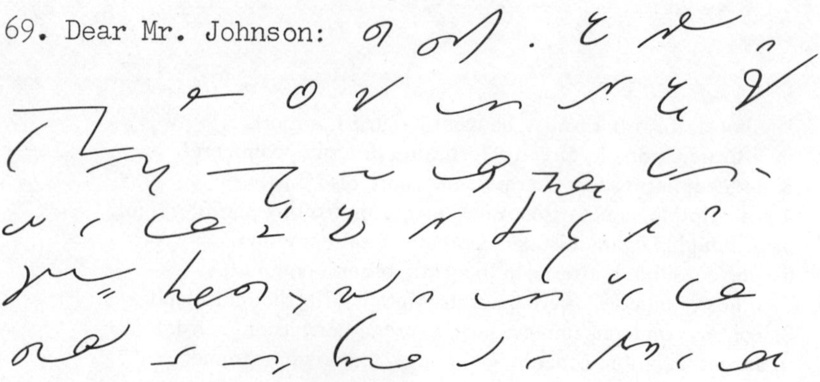

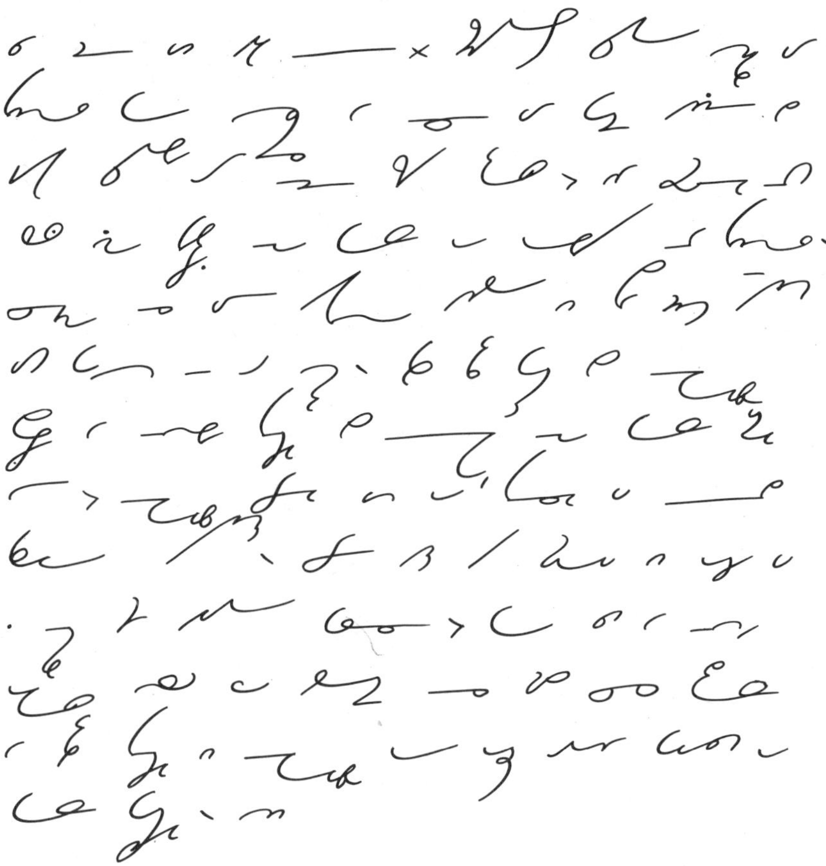

70. Dear Miss Carter: 

71. Mr. Forman:

72. THE COMPETENT SECRETARY SAVES THE EMPLOYER'S TIME

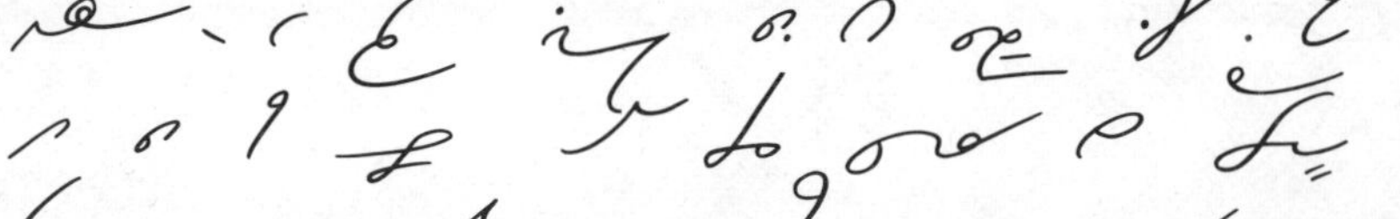

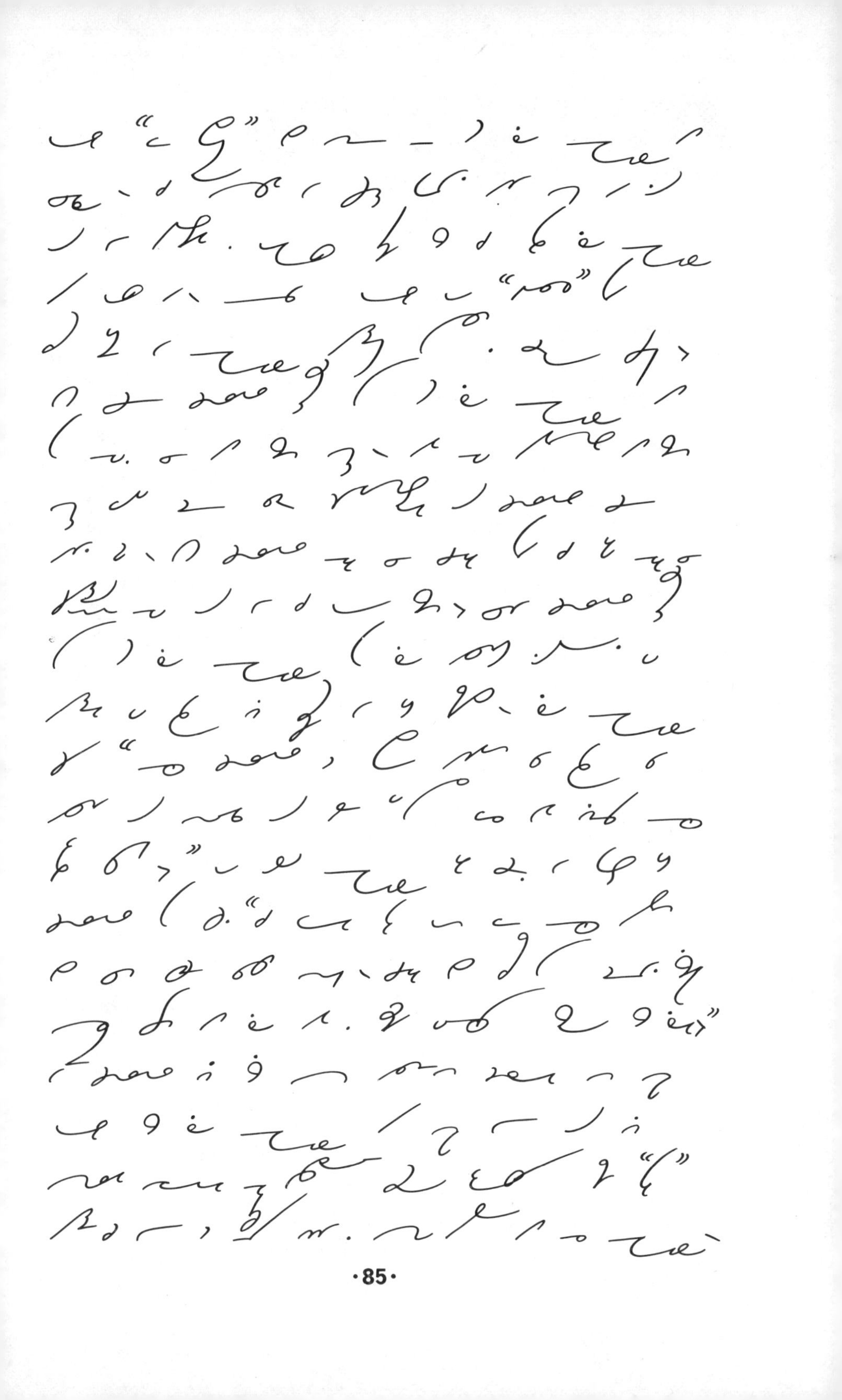

LESSON 18

PRINCIPLES

The following chart contains all the *joined* word endings.

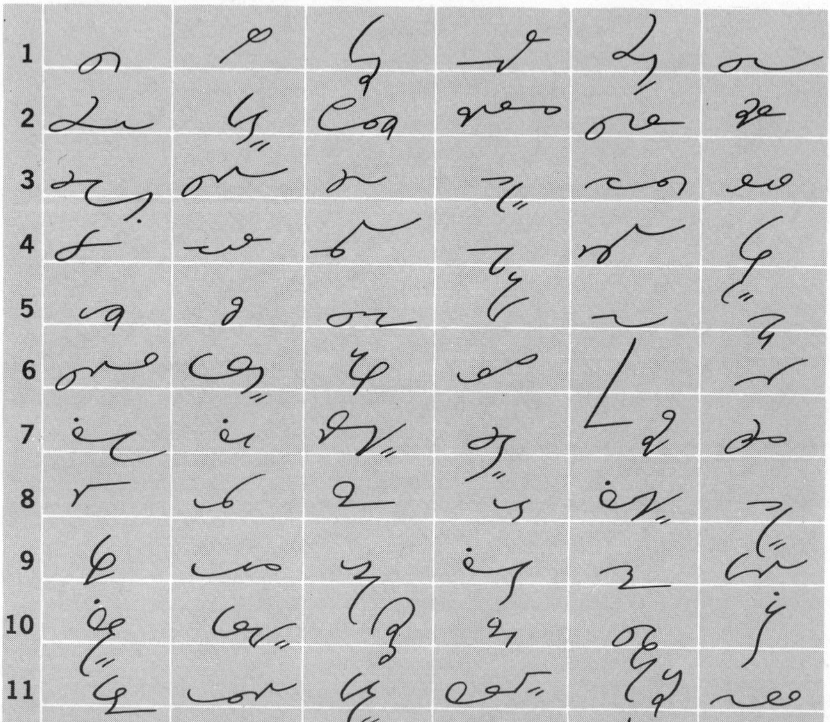

1. action, daily, beneficial, modern, verified, annual.
2. failure, Pittsfield, application, extremely, agreement, western.
3. simplifying, actual, secure, Newport, collection, thoroughly.
4. payment, northern, needless, impose, schedule, Bridgeport.
5. occasion, easily, announcement, obtain, unless, composition.
6. actually, Plainfield, operation, readily, judgment, contain.
7. helpless, herself, Stamford, Zanesville, efficient, finally.
8. statement, retain, assume, ourselves, Hartford, Newburgh.
9. patient, locally, reasonable, helpful, consume, picture.

10. Harrisburg, Princeton, deficiency, essential, acceptable, hopeful.
11. presume, lecture, Pittsburgh, Allentown, official, clearly.
12. advisable, useful, resumption, nature, Jacksonville, Nashville.
13. early, initial, desirable, modify, resumed, procured.

FREQUENTLY USED WORDS

Here are 40 additional words of high frequency.

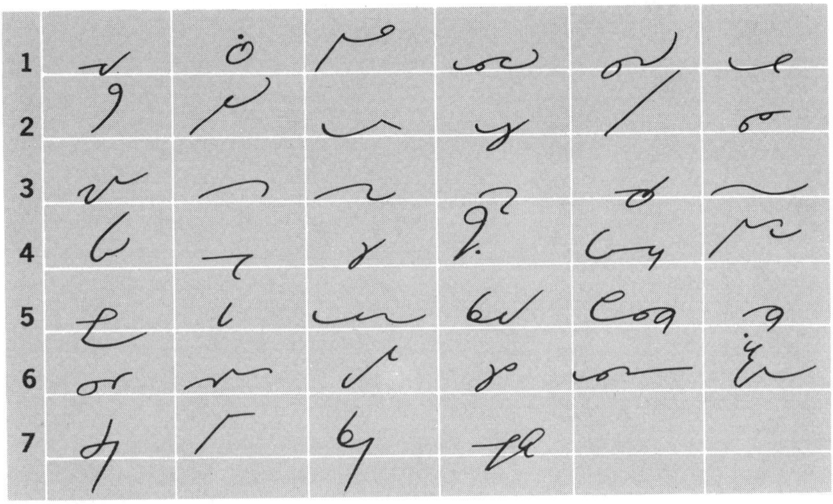

1. note, high, delivery, record, account, less.
2. ever, don't, long, receipt, did, within.
3. water, go, great, keep, night, glad.
4. both, important, set, advertising, promotion, director.
5. national, show, local, period, application, case.
6. another, contract, orders, city, recommend, hospital.
7. change, done, charge, merchandise.

READING AND SELF-DICTATION PRACTICE

73. Dear Member:

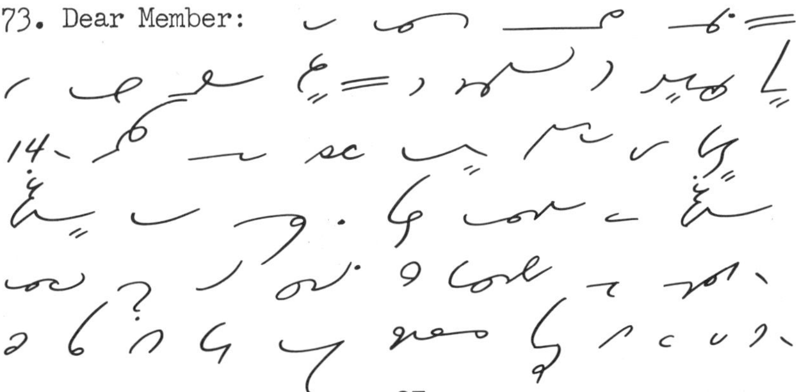

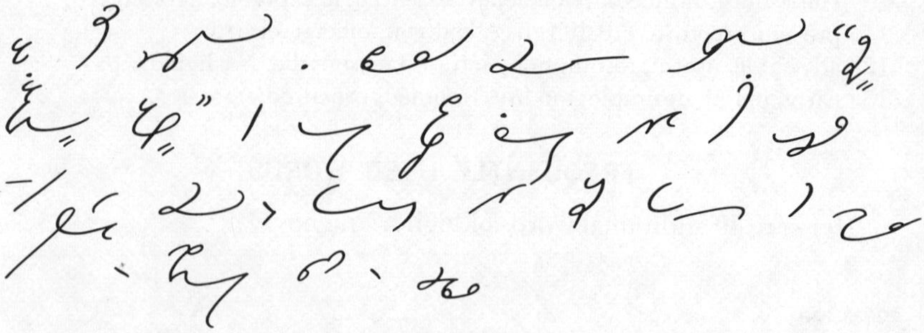

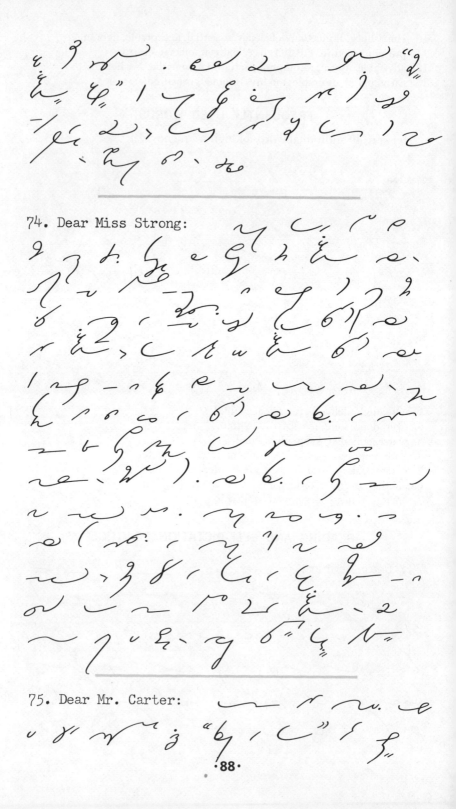

74. Dear Miss Strong: 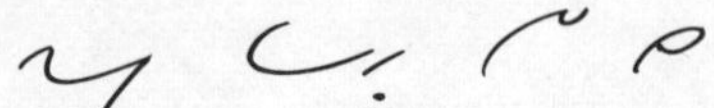

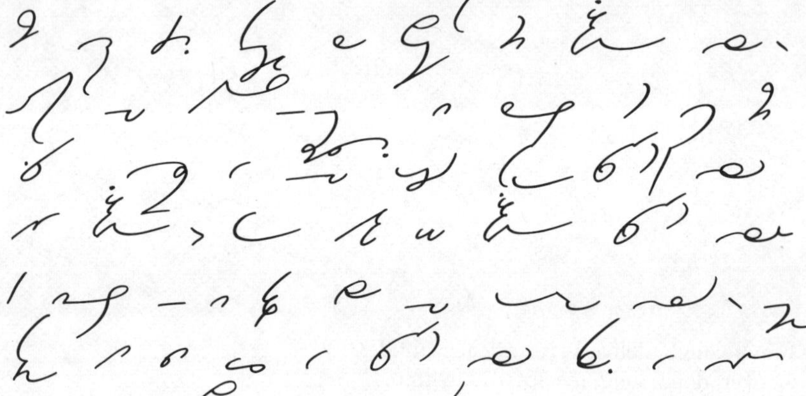

75. Dear Mr. Carter: 

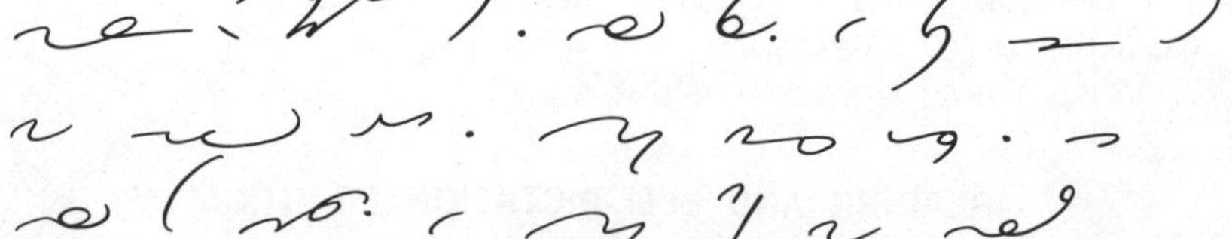

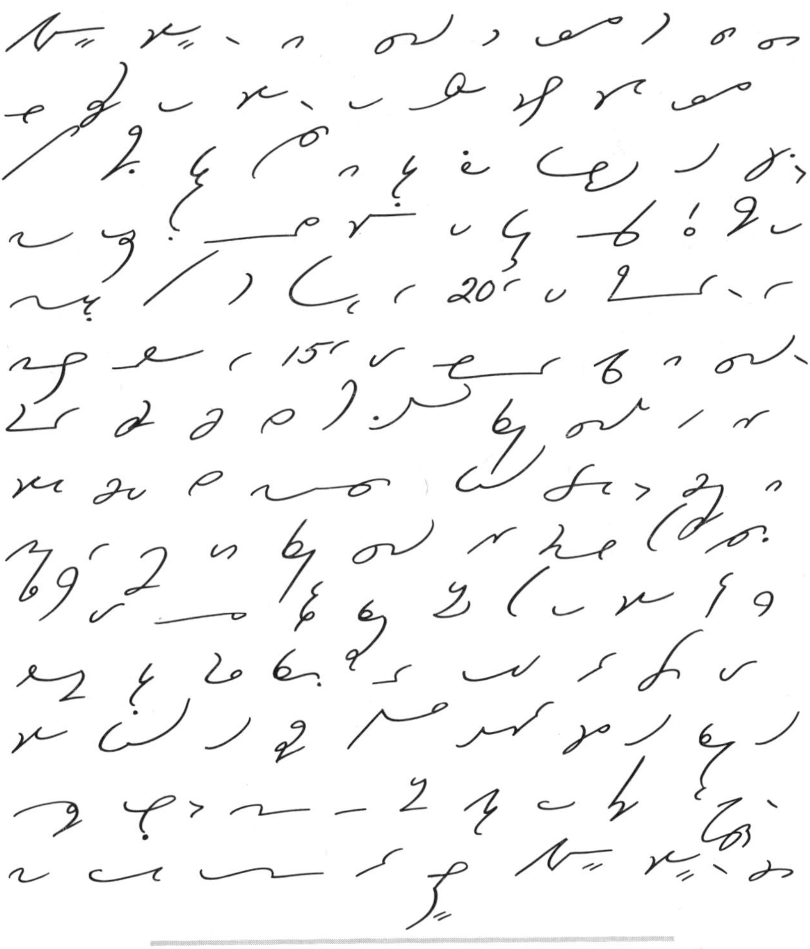

76. Dear Mr. Adams: 

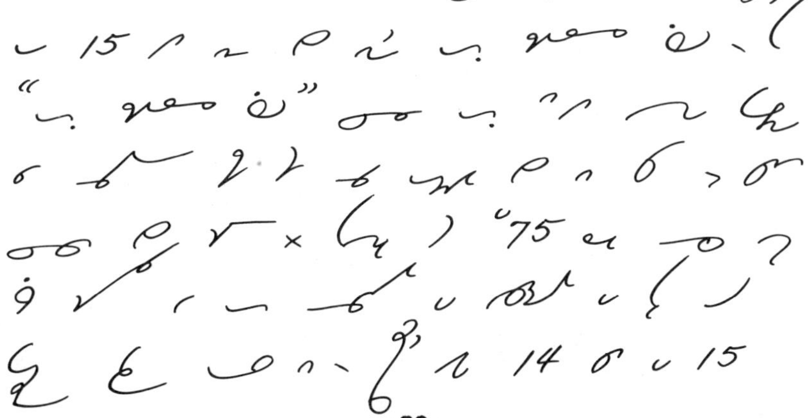

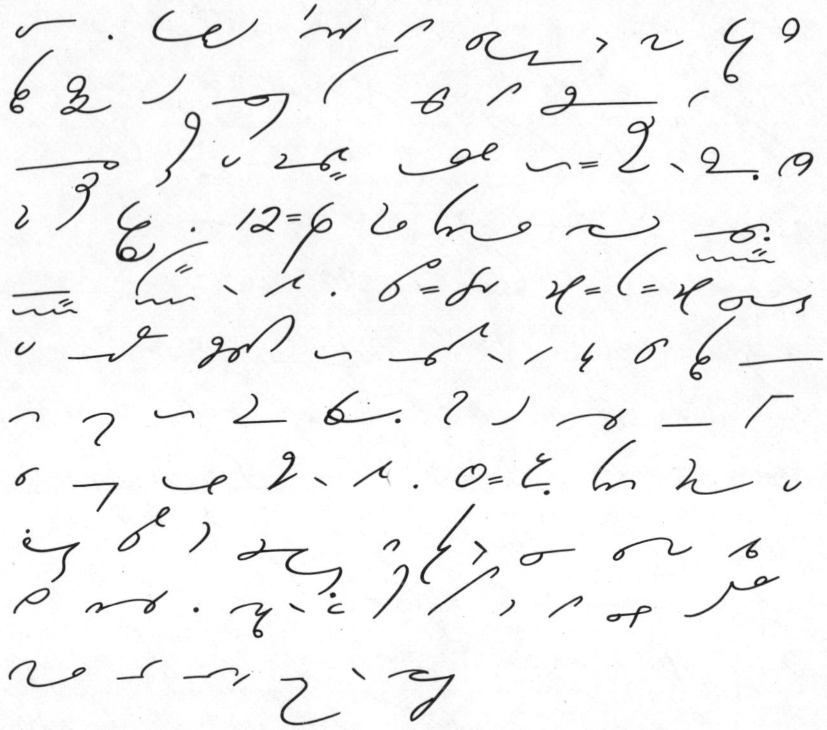

77. Gentlemen:

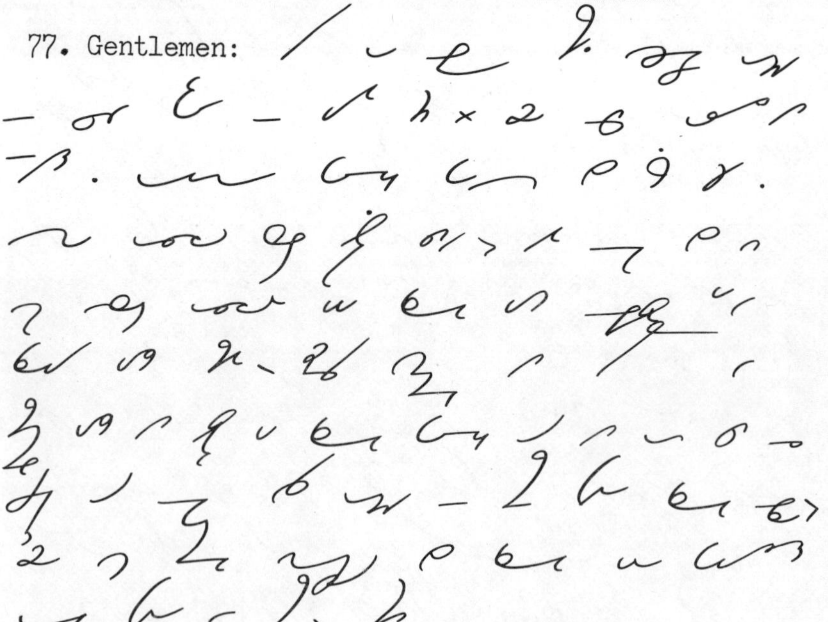

LESSON 19

PRINCIPLES

The following chart contains all the *disjoined* word beginnings and endings.

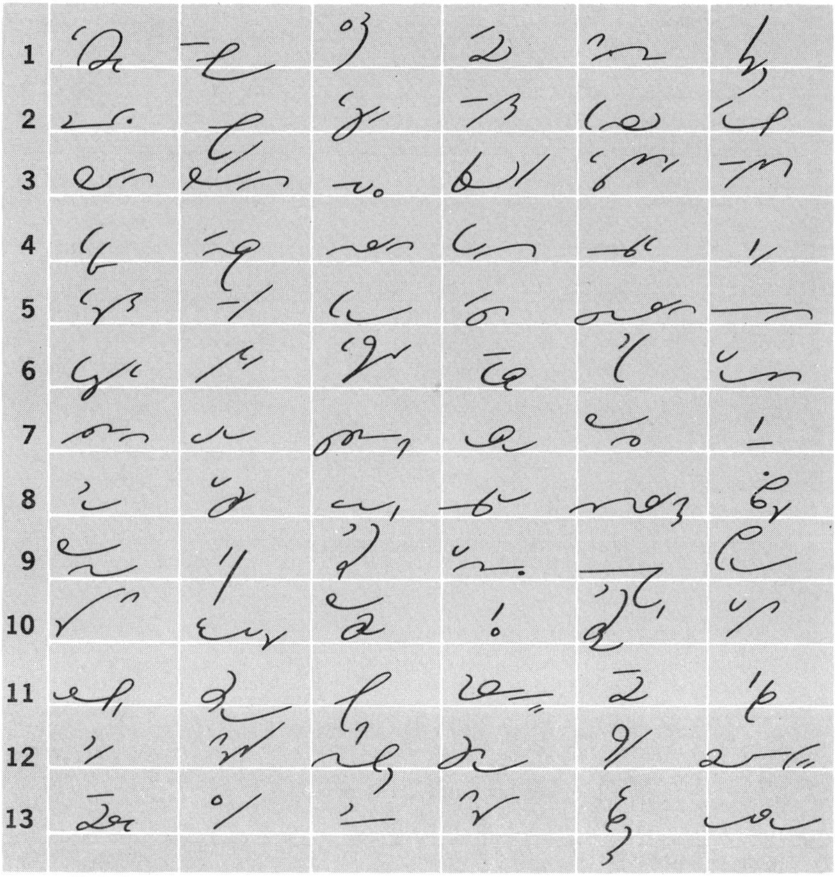

1. self-defense, international, inclusive, transferred, undergone, justification.
2. something, neighborhood, self-satisfied, introduce, postcard, translation.
3. article, telegram, knowingly, childhood, self-educated, introduction.
4. postpone, transcribe, critical, program, meetings, shipped.
5. circumstances, entered, postal, transact, analytical, monogram.
6. proceedings, desired, self-evident, enterprise, superb, overlook.
7. technical, authority, accumulation, writer, electrically, shorten.

8. superior, oversight, ownership, maturity, congratulations, happiest.
9. electrical, shortage, supervision, overcoming, membership, ability.
10. stimulate, slowest, electric wire, shortly, supervisor, overdue.
11. relationship, facility, tabulation, Framingham, interfere, shipshape.
12. support, understood, classification, faculty, afterward, Wilmington.
13. interference, include, supreme, understand, specifications, loyalty.

FREQUENTLY USED WORDS

Here is another group of 40 words of high frequency.

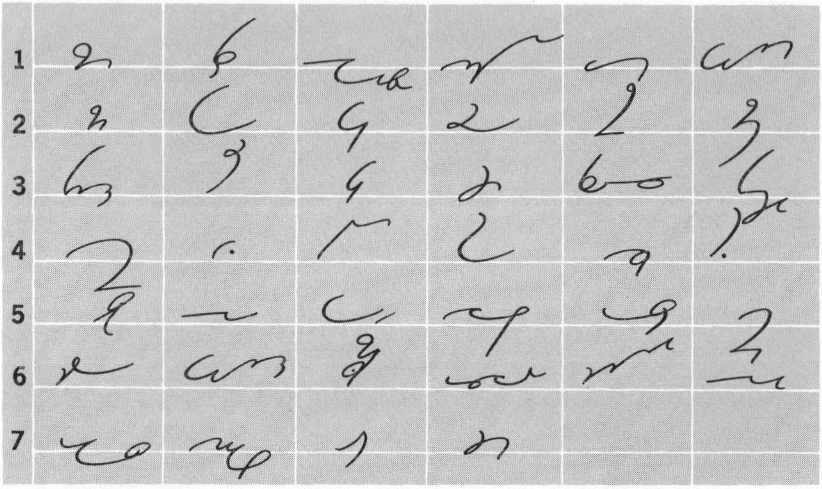

1. ask, basis, employees, customer, organization, production.
2. issue, bill, purchase, fill, even, effective.
3. books, several, position, fact, chairman, benefits.
4. government, think, direct, value, cash, having.
5. type, market, pleased, college, life, convention.
6. still, products, association, records, students, Mrs.
7. reply, cooperation, therefore, section.

READING AND SELF-DICTATION PRACTICE

78. HOW TO GET A PROMOTION

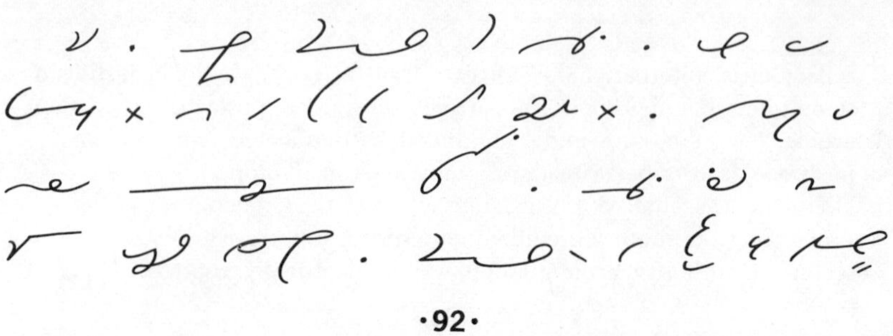

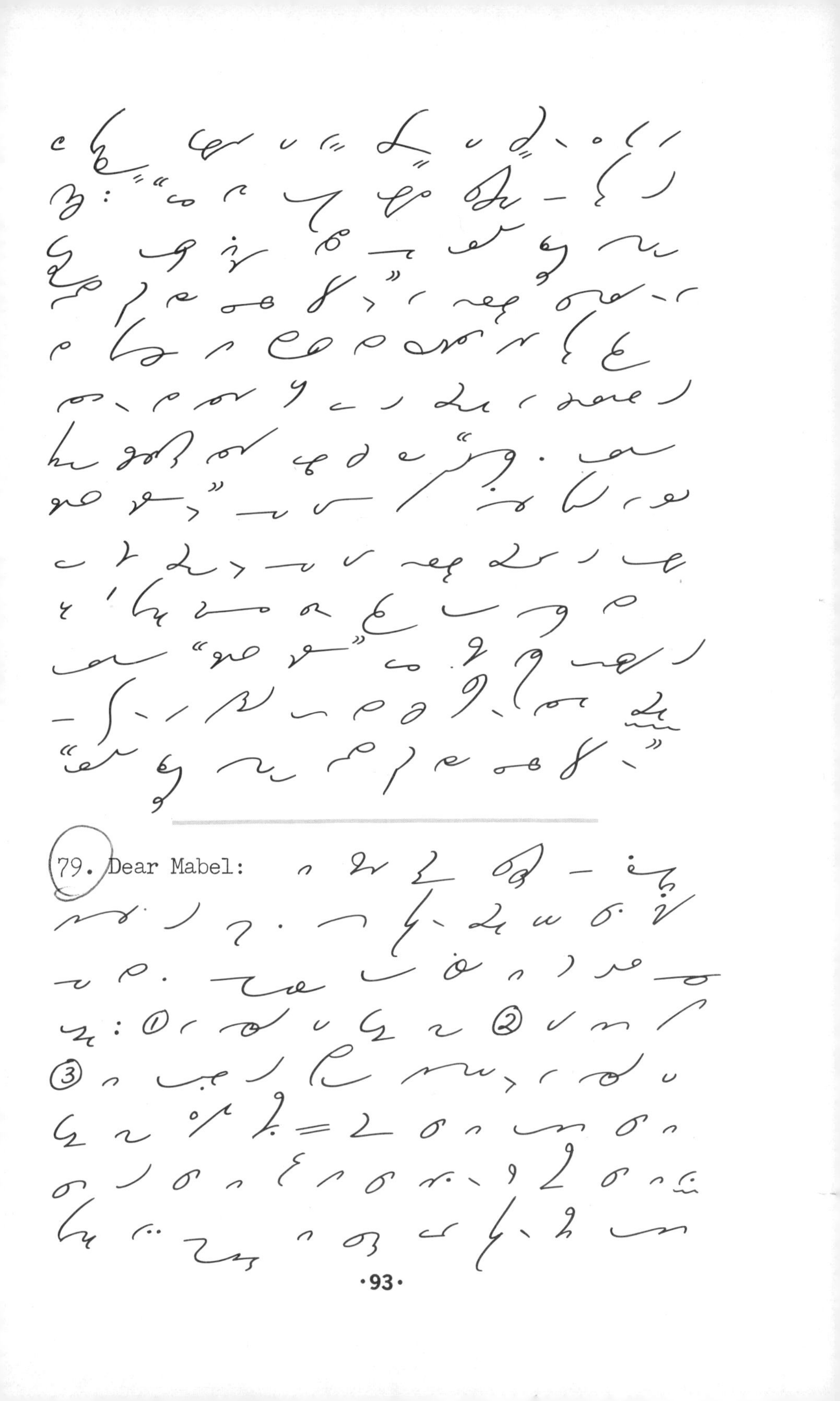

79. Dear Mabel:

80. Dear Mr. Cunningham:

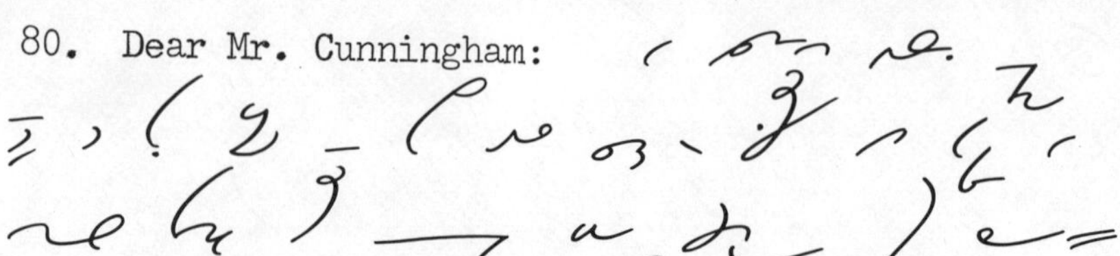

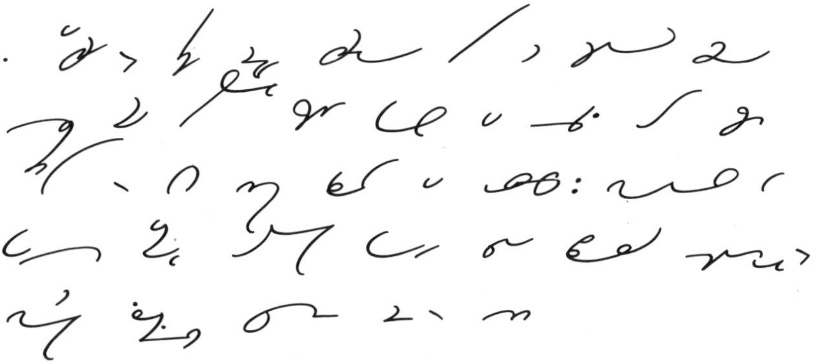

81. Dear Mr. Ballard: 

82. Dear Mr. Murdock: 

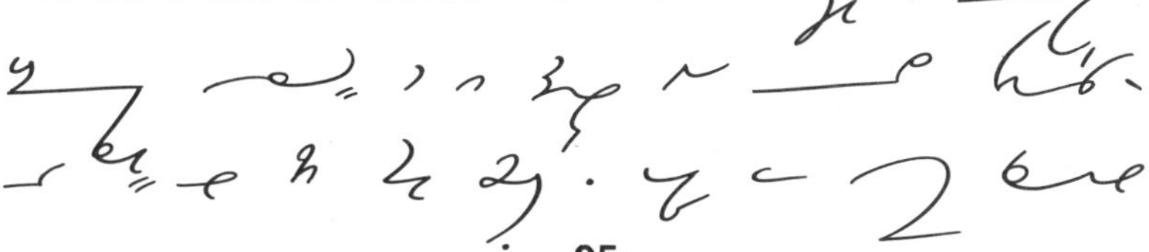

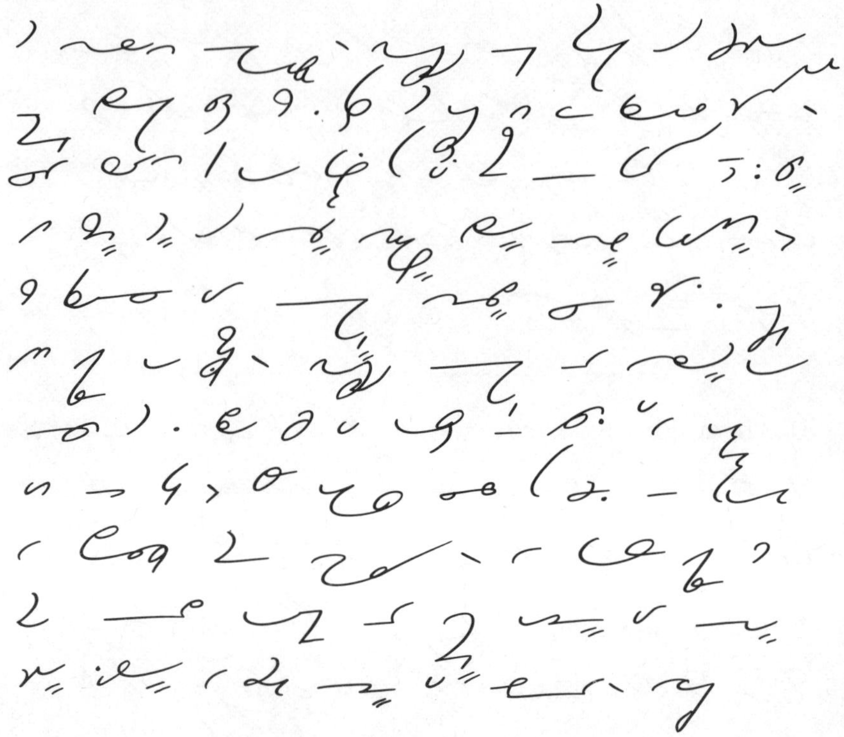

83. Dear Mrs. Cummings:

LESSON 20

PRINCIPLES

The following chart contains all the blends and illustrates the omission of vowels and consonants.

1. examine, credit, prevent, filed, difference, maintain.
2. competition, announce, many, editor, friend, mailed.
3. positive, obtain, condition, news, memo, quoted.
4. signed, dependable, creative, certain, permission, reduce.
5. mental, deduction, entire, expenditure, acceptance, attempt.
6. donation, report, mention, steady, entry, spent.
7. attention, custom, foundation, modern, monthly, united.

8. empty, happened, tonight, estimate, summons, active.
9. minimum, apparent, seemed, urgent, written, system.
10. funds, exactly, memory, center, prompt, gentle.
11. audience, damage, town, motor, manager, client.
12. heard, definite, evidence, demonstration, down, insist.
13. needed, event, harder, develop, sudden, demand.

FREQUENTLY USED WORDS

Here is the last group of 40 words of high frequency.

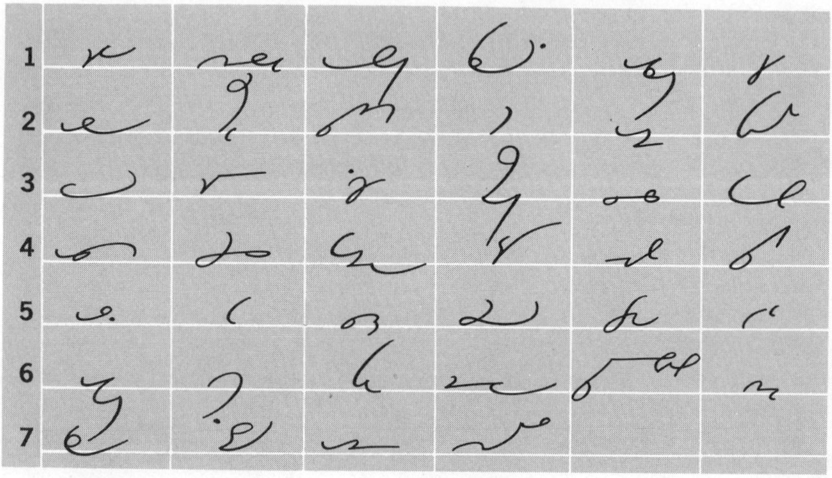

1. store, commerce, large, building, reserve, sheet.
2. real, savings, education, four, reason, bonds.
3. old, statement, whether, average, immediately, place.
4. regular, family, personal, system, notice, addition.
5. regarding, put, weeks, field, power, thanks.
6. representative, covering, box, small, administration, once.
7. sale, assistant, room, country.

READING AND SELF-DICTATION PRACTICE

84. SECRETARIAL ATTRIBUTES

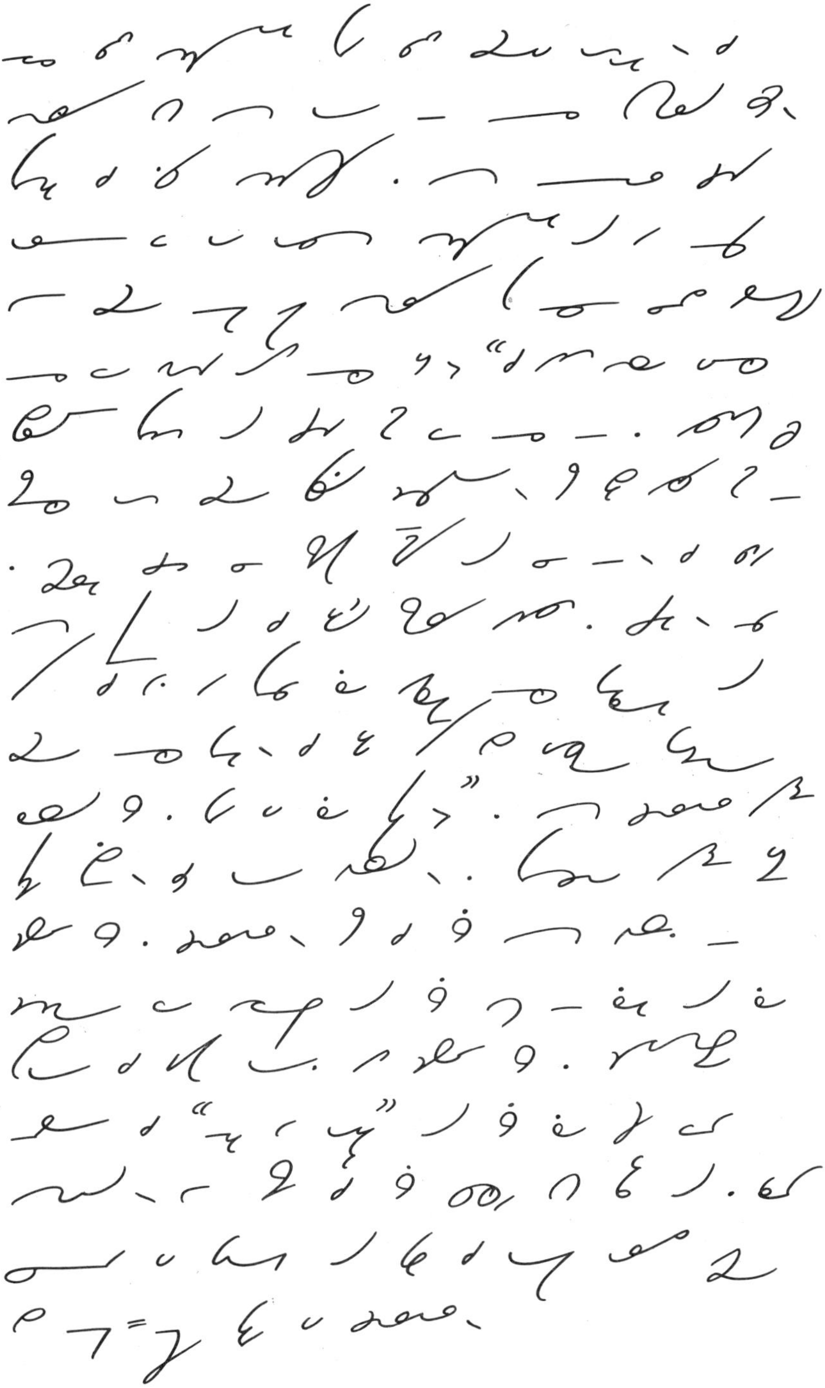

85. Dear Neighbor: 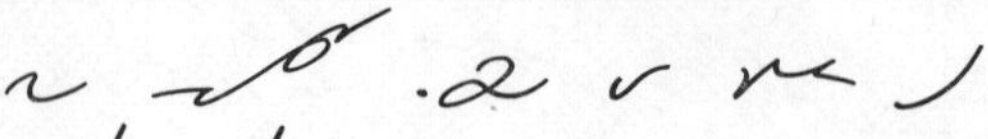

86. Dear Mrs. Bennett: 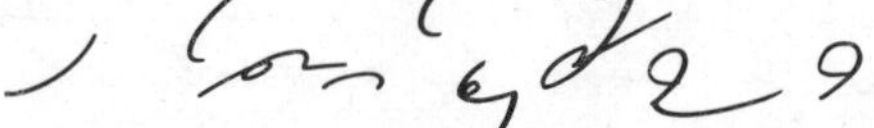

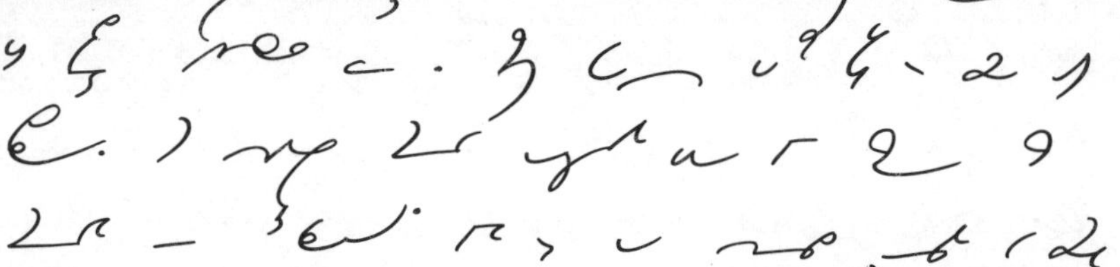

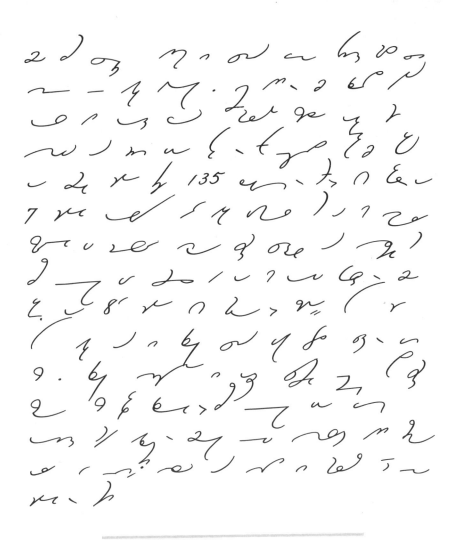

87. Dear Alumnus:

WHERE TO FROM HERE?

Now that you have completed a comprehensive review of the principles of Gregg Shorthand, you are ready to further enhance that skill through a dictation practice program.

The ability to take verbatim office dictation, according to a research conducted by Dr. H. H. Green requires a "cruising" speed of 80 to 100 words a minute, with speed spurts between 120 and 140 words a minute. To be certain of a "new matter" speed of 100 words a minute, you will want to bring your speed on practiced material – letters or articles that you have previously read in shorthand or recorded dictation that you have taken several times – to at least 120 words a minute.

Remember that the greater dictation speed you attain the greater the confidence you will have in your ability, and the better you will perform.

DON'T LET THIS HAPPEN TO YOU!

DICTATED

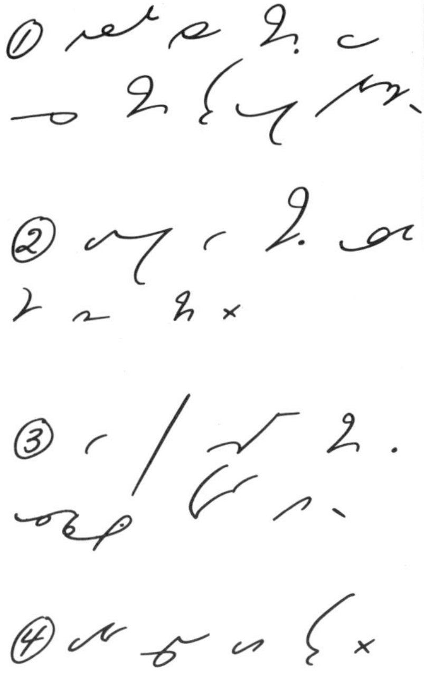

1. Trends that are *affecting* or may *affect* business will be discussed.

2. What will be the advertising rates for the *one* issue?

3. The judge could not *effect* a reconciliation between the two.

4. What is the *nature* of your business?

TRANSCRIBED

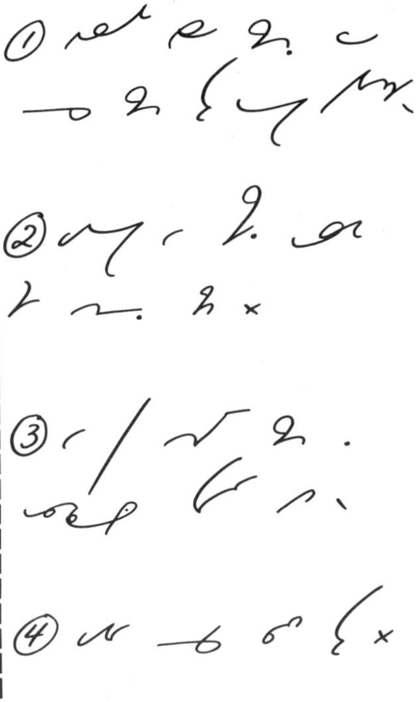

1. Trends that are *asking* or may *ask* business will be discussed.

2. What will be the advertising rates for the *coming* issue?

3. The judge could not *ask* a reconciliation between the two.

4. What is the *matter* with your business?

KEY TO READING AND SELF-DICTATION PRACTICE

(The material is counted in groups of 20 standard words or 28 syllables for convenience in timing the reading or dictation.)

Lesson 1, Page 2

1. Mr. Hale: May I bring in my car for repairs one day during the coming week? There are several things that need[1] to be done, and I have been lax in taking care of them. I know that I need a new spare tire, for the old one is[2] so worn that it must be replaced. Too, there are a number of chips in the paint that need to be looked after. The[3] important thing, however, is that you fix the brakes. I am afraid to drive the car in its present condition. As[4] you know, my territory includes all of James County. Many of the roads in this county are not paved, and on[5] steep grades driving can be dangerous.

Would you check with the mechanic to find out whether there is any chance that[6] I might have this work done on Wednesday, May 27? I should like to know so that I can make my plans. If the[7] work will take longer than a day to finish, then I shall have to hire a car in order to cover my[8] territory.

Please let me hear from you soon. Perhaps you would like to telephone me, or you may write me if you desire.[9] I will be at home the rest of this week. Cordially yours, (190)

2. Dear Harry: Could you give me the names and addresses of the people who will be staying at the Clear Lake Motel[1] during our club meeting beginning March 15? I must make reservations for rooms immediately. I[2] believe the motel will give us a special rate of $7 plus tax. This rate seems reasonable, don't you think?[3] All rooms are with bath and telephone.

Are the papers you were to prepare being typed? I am relying on you[4] to have them ready for the meeting. I know it is not an easy job, and I am glad that no one gave it to[5] me! Will you be able to attend the meetings? It will help a great deal if you are there, as you are perhaps the[6] only one who will be able to answer all the questions that may be asked.

I am attaching the list of new[7] members that Mary Grady gave me. Have you seen it? Did you know that she is writing a history of the club?[8] George (161)

3. Dear Mr. Harrison: Your most important asset is your health. Are you taking good care of it? Or, like many[1] others, are you putting off having a health examination because you feel the bill will be too high? If so,[2] we have good news for you.

Our new Three-Way Health Plan does three important things for you: It gives you a thorough[3] examination three times a year by skilled doctors; it gives you home treatment when you need it; and it provides complete[4] hospital benefits. This new plan has become so well known that more than ten thousand people have joined it during the[5] last three months. Yet the fees are very small.

The enclosed booklet explains the plan fully. You owe it to yourself to[6] read it carefully. Why not telephone us this week and arrange to visit our office so that we can explain[7] more completely the benefits of joining the Three-Way Plan. You will be glad you did. Cordially yours, (158)

4. Dear Friend: Do you take chances when you drive? "Of course not!" you say. Yet each one of us takes chances when we are not[1] prepared for winter driving.

The smart driver does not take chances when driving in sleet, ice, or snow. He makes sure he has[2] a set of Atlas chains in his car during the winter season.

The car owner who has Atlas chains knows that he[3] has nothing to worry about even in the worst weather. These chains snap on easily, and they grip icy roads[4] like a vise—no fear of accidents or delays.

Please look at the attached report on drivers who have used Atlas[5] chains. Do not take unnecessary risks. Get your set of Atlas chains today. Cordially yours, (117)

5. To Branch Managers: You all did such a good job at the party last Friday that I wish to take this way of thanking[1] each of you. I never saw a group pitch in more eagerly.

I would like particularly to comment on[2] the decorations; the effect was so startling that I thought they were arranged by a professional. Mrs. Chase[3] said she would like to take lessons in flower arrangements from the decoration committee.

The food was so[4] beautifully displayed that it would have given anyone an appetite. A number of our guests thought that we had[5] a caterer supply the food. When I told them that you people had done everything, they could scarcely believe[6] it. So thanks once more. F. C. Chase (126)

Lesson 2, Page 7

6. Dear Madam: May we have the opportunity of showing you our new Store-Away filing cabinets for the[1] home? Perhaps you saw them advertised in the *Daily News* on Wednesday and Thursday of last week. They will be on display[2] at the Wilson branch of our store, 226 Broadway, on Friday, November 7.

Those who have seen these[3] smart filing cabinets have expressed delight with their beauty and efficiency. You will be pleased, too, with their modern[4] styling. And what is more, they do not waste space; they save space for you. The manufacturers of Store-Away filing[5] cabinets have made files for business firms for many years; businesses all over the country have purchased them.[6] We feel fortunate that we are the first in the city to feature these files, which are designed expressly for the[7] home.

A special demonstration of these files will be given on Friday at 2:30 P.M. I hope you will[8] be able to come for at least a quick visit. Cordially yours, (172)

7. Dear Wade: We are pleased to send you the sales analysis that we have just completed, using the figures that you[1] supplied us recently. We sincerely hope that we have set up this information the way you want it. If we[2] have not, it is essential that we hear from you not later than Tuesday of next week in order to make any[3] changes in time for your board meeting.

As for the additional material that we promised you, we will get[4] it to you before the end of December. Please be patient with us. Cordially yours, (95)

8. Dear Mr. Wooley: Your copy of our new marketing bulletin is in the mail. We know that you will find it[1] of great help in planning your fall campaign. Every year we say, "This is the best bulletin we have ever[2] prepared"; and again we feel that this year's bulletin is much better than any we have ever had before. We[3] feel sure that you will be pleased and will like the special features that appear at the end of each section.

We take pride[4] in the fact that during the past fifty years we have been able to supply our bulletins at a very low[5] price. However, this particular issue is the first that we have been able to offer for less than[6] 75 cents. You will be glad to learn that we can supply you with any number you wish.

To be assured of getting[7] your copies while they are still available, fill in the enclosed form and return it to us quickly. Your order[8] will receive prompt action. Yours truly, (167)

9. Dear Mrs. Quimby: You are invited to the grand opening of our new store. Our business has grown so much in[1] the past two years that we have had to move to larger, more efficient quarters. Our new location is 125[2] Queens Boulevard.

All types of woolens are to be featured on the opening day; the second day we will feature[3] nylons and Dacrons; the third day we will emphasize accessories of all kinds.

The enclosed picture story[4] will give you a partial idea of just what we have planned. We also have some delightful surprises that we would[5] rather not mention at this time. Come and find out for yourself!

We hope that you will be able to join us on[6] Saturday, June 16. Cordially yours, (127)

10. Dear Cousin Carol: In my previous letter to you I said that, on the whole, I like this vacation spot[1] better than any other I have ever visited. The mornings and nights are very cool; the days are warm but not[2] hot. I have only five precious days left, and I shall be sorry when my vacation ends.

When I get home, I'll explain[3] to you and Bruce Moore why I did not come back last Saturday for the Social Club dance. It's a long story. Did[4] I tell you that Homer and Bill drove up here last Sunday? Homer borrowed his sister's car for the trip.

Don't wait long[5] to drop me a line. I do want to hear from you again. Sincerely, (113)

Lesson 3, Page 12

11. Dear Mr. Field: Perhaps some of your friends are planning to retire at 60 with a monthly income of[1] $300. Will you be able to do so, too—or will you barely manage to

get by? Research shows that[2] surprisingly few people plan ahead for retirement. It will be to your advantage to start saving toward retirement[3] now. We can help you. How?

Read the enclosure that I am sending with this letter. The information it[4] contains is worth much to you and your family. After you have had a chance to study the features of our[5] retirement plan, we will be pleased to receive a telephone call from you about arranging for a personal[6] meeting. You will be under no obligation whatsoever. Cordially yours, (134)

12. Dear Mr. Arnold: We should like to send you information about the new family insurance plan that is[1] causing so much excitement among those who hear about it.

Now it is possible for your entire family[2] to be covered under a single protection plan. Any new children in your family will be insured[3] as soon as they are ten days old, and there will be no increase in the rates thereafter. I think you will readily[4] see that this is a totally new concept of family insurance.

Please do not make the mistake of waiting[5] until trouble arrives in the form of illness and emergencies. If you have no insurance protection, you[6] owe it to yourself to let us show you how easy and inexpensive it is to protect your family and[7] your income under our new family insurance plan.

May our representative, Mr. Childs, call on you to[8] describe the features of this unique insurance plan? He will gladly do so if you will telephone him—the number[9] is Worth 2-4121. Cordially yours, (189)

13. Dear Mr. Blake: I am very pleased to send you our new catalogue featuring the latest models of the Cold[1] King Coolers. You will notice that we have added two new models to our line—the compact Neptune and the roomy[2] North Wind. Those who have purchased these popular coolers (over 3,000 of each have already been sold) say that[3] they have not had a single repair bill. We are convinced that these are the finest low-priced coolers on the market.[4] The Neptune retails for $16.95; the North Wind, for $22.95.

We[5] are glad to be able to offer you a special discount of 25 per cent instead of your usual[6] 20 per cent on all Cold King Coolers. This discount is available only during the months of February,[7] March, and April; therefore, you must act quickly. Delivery will be made within two weeks after your order[8] is received, yet you will not be billed for sixty days. Over 100,000 customers can't be wrong! Order[9] your supply of Cold King Coolers today and get ready for big spring and summer business. Sincerely yours, (198)

14. Dear Subscriber: When we wrote you in January that we would be very pleased to renew your subscription to[1] *United Business* and that it was not necessary to send money at that time, we told you that we[2] would bill you in February.

We sent you the bill, but we have not as yet heard from you. We do not feel that you have intentionally[3] ignored our correspondence; it is likely that this small bill has slipped your mind. If so, may we have your[4] check in the enclosed envelope. No stamp is needed. If, however, your remittance has been mailed, please ignore this[5] reminder. Cordially yours, (105)

Lesson 4, Page 17

15. Dear Mr. Franklin: On Tuesday, August 10, I shall be meeting with Keith Yale from Cleveland. Mr. Yale, who was[1] one of your students, is applying for a position in our bank's bookkeeping department. His school record is[2] highly satisfactory, and we thank you for sending it. Would you also answer a few questions concerning[3] him? Please be very frank.

Did he get along well with the teachers and others in your school? Was he able to take[4] criticism? Did he hold any important offices? Did he turn in his work on time? Was his attendance[5] satisfactory? Was he a hard worker? If Mr. Yale were to apply to you for a position, would you[6] hire him?

Whatever information you give us will be held in strict confidence, of course. Cordially yours, (139)

16. Dear Mr. White: I have been thinking a great deal about you. You are one of the people for whom I have been[1] working for many years, because, through the pages of Family Picture Magazine, I try to bring inspiration[2] and help to parents such as you.

Actually, as editor of the magazine, I have met only a[3] few of our readers face to face. How then, you may ask, do I know what they like and don't like in a family[4] magazine? I have learned to realize that the hopes and fears of parents in bringing up their children—whether the are[5] youngsters of four or youths of fourteen – are much like the hopes and fears I have in bringing up my own children. That is[6] why I try to gather helpful and important guidance tips and feature them in every issue of the[7] magazine.

To make it easy for you to renew your subscription, I am sending along a renewal blank.[8] Sincerely yours, (162)

17. Dear Mrs. Jackson: The national convention of the Yachting Association meets at the Overman Hotel[1] in New Orleans on May 16 and 17. Delegates from every chapter in the country will[2] attend. The delegates from Michigan and Pennsylvania chapters planned the program; Oregon and New York[3] delegates are in charge of social activities and sports events.

Your chapter has not yet expressed a desire to[4] participate in any particular activity. Won't you look over the enclosed list and let us know[5] your preferences? We particularly need help with the yacht races and other sports events. Will your chapter[6] volunteer its services?

I shall be looking forward to hearing from you soon. Thank you very much. Cordially[7] yours, (141)

18. Dear Mr. Long: We are having a very unusual sale of leather goods beginning December[1] 26. Although Christmas will have come and gone by the time this sale starts, many wise buyers actually[2] purchase their Christmas gifts as much as a year in advance. That is what we are suggesting to you.

I am sure that if[3] you stop in to see us during the week of December 26, you will find many worthwhile leather gifts[4] on display. In addition, we shall be featuring quite an assortment of other gift ideas—linens from Ireland,[5] furniture from Spain, and porcelain from Italy. You are sure to see something that will please your mother, father,[6] and the entire family.

We shall look for you during our sale. Cordially yours, (134)

Lesson 5, Page 21

19. Dear Mr. Weeks: As one of our valued stockholders, you are entitled to know the latest developments in[1] the story of the Universal Brush Company. If you have seen our recent financial statement, you know that[2] we have been making marvelous progress in our efforts to increase our business.

Recently, we merged with the World[3] Products Corporation, which distributes various supplies for the home. I realize that there are those groups who[4] warn small companies of the dangers of bigness—that it is likely to weaken our position. I am unable[5] to understand why this is a problem. We feel that this merger will automatically give us many advantages:[6]

1. It will enable our customers to choose from a wider variety of products at an even[7] higher quality.

2. Fast, courteous treatment of all customers will be possible.

3. We have more capital[8] with which to expand our services and our operations.

4. In this merger, we have acquired[9] many outstanding people. As you know, we have always wanted wider market coverage, and this expansion[10] of personnel will give it to us.

5. Faster methods of shipment will be available to us. Distance is[11] no longer a problem and damaged merchandise should be cut to a minimum.

On the basis of this evidence,[12] I am sure you will agree that this merger with World was a wise thing. We estimate that our volume will more than[13] double in the coming year. Yes, we are getting big, and we hope to get even bigger!

I hope you will be pleased[14] with this new development at Universal. We are very excited about it ourselves and have gone to[15] a great deal of trouble to make sure it was the right thing for us to do. After the coming year you can judge for[16] yourself. As always, we welcome your reactions. Individual stockholders such as you are, after all, the[17] people who are most concerned. Write us today, tomorrow, or next month. We shall be glad to hear from you. Sincerely[18] yours, (361)

20. Dear Mrs. Swift: They say that if you want to get something done, give it to a busy person. We desperately[1] need to get something done, and, as usual, we are looking to you for leadership.

The first PTA meeting[2] of the year will be held at Cummings High School next week—Thursday evening, October 10. This meeting will be divided[3] into two parts—a business session from 7:30 to 8:30, and a "fun hour" from 8:30 to 9:30.[4]

We particularly need your guidance at the business session. We are organizing several committees[5] for the summer and for the next school year. Because of your knowledge and experience in committee work, we are[6] hoping that you will be available to assist at this meeting.

We do want you to know that during the last[7] hour you can sit back with the audience and enjoy the fun, as the teachers are putting on a skit called "Who Am[8] I?" This title promises a good show, and we expect a large audience for it.

May I please have your acceptance?[9] Possibly you can telephone me at Freedom 3-1612, Extension 218. Sincerely yours,[10] (200)

21. Dear Mrs. Lane: Thank you very much for your recent letter inviting me to participate in the PTA[1] meeting on October 10 at Cummings High School. My answer is "Yes."

I have several important suggestions[2] in mind, which I would like to talk over with you some morning before October 10, if that is convenient[3] with you.

I have been seriously interested for many years in the field of mental health. Mental disease[4] in young people is a great problem, and treatment is slow and expensive. I would, therefore, be pleased for the[5] opportunity to work on the mental hygiene committee. We can discuss the idea in your office in advance[6] of October 10, if you are able to set a date. Sincerely yours, P.S. By the way, Mr. Swift will be[7] at the meeting with me. (144)

22. To the Staff: Good news! In the future, Washington's Birthday (February 22) will be a holiday[1] for the employees of our company. Since it falls on a Sunday this year, we shall be observing the holiday[2] on Monday. We wanted to get this bulletin to you in advance so that you might plan for the long weekend.[3]

We have been asked by the Travel Club to announce that arrangements are being made for a special bus to Mountain[4] Springs. It will leave the building at 4:30 Friday and return to the city at noon Monday, February[5] 23. To obtain further information, call Miss Summers on Extension 2651. J. H. Harris[6] (120)

Lesson 6, Page 27

23. Dear Mr. Royal: As a merchant in the Windy City, you are, of course, proud of the progress that is now being[1] made in road improvement in the entire state, as well as in Chicago. These better roads will bring more business[2] to Chicago and you want to share in it.

We would like you to study the United Merchandising Plan. Its[3] purpose is to help you sell more at less expense; and less expense means a greater net profit for you. Here are just[4] a few of our services:

1. We maintain a staff who will see that your windows are trimmed each month.

2. You can use[5] our credit to purchase additional merchandise.

3. You'll save on direct-mail printing costs the United way.[6]

4. We have an outlet store that will relieve you of soiled merchandise at a reasonable discount.

Why not take a[7] few minutes to read our offer. If, after a careful study of the details, you wish to have any of[8] these services explained more fully, we shall send one of our representatives to tell you about the progress[9] you can make the United way.

If you feel no further explanation is needed, the enclosed contract signed[10] by you is all that is necessary—we'll do the rest. Yours truly, (213)

24. Dear Mr. Conant: When I was browsing in your store last week while waiting for you to make up my order, I noticed[1] some empty boxes standing in a corner.

My church is having a fair next month and could use such boxes as[2] these to pack merchandise sold at the fair. I will be glad to pick up the boxes, along with anything else[3] you might consider donating for such a worthy cause. Of course, anything you donate will[4] be tax-exempt. Cordially yours, (86)

25. Dear Roy: I am remaining in Philadelphia two or three days longer than I planned. There has been some difficulty[1] with the tenants on our property here.

A few of the tenants claimed they had not signed their leases because[2] a study made by the city council might result in a widening of the street. In that event, they explained, they[3] thought the property might be sold.

I doubt that was the reason, but I find it difficult and annoying to handle[4] such details. Ordinarily, I take care of such matters myself; but today I have retained a real estate[5] firm to try to straighten out the difficulty.

As I mentioned to you, I plan to go on to Detroit and[6] then to Chicago to review the progress that has been made in maintaining family properties in those cities.[7] Then I will go on to California.

As soon as I return to my office, I'll get in touch with you. Cordially[8] yours, (161)

26. Dear Mr. Temple: You inquired about our Alabama link-chain fence. As described in the booklet I sent[1] you, this fence is more secure than the ordinary fence. Why? It is much heavier. This means that you can trust it[2] to keep your children inside and stray animals outside.

As to its purchase – that's easy. The enclosed brochure explains[3] the monthly time-payment plan. If you place your orders promptly, you will be exempt from monthly payments until fall.[4]

This fence is one you will be proud to own; and in addition to its attractive appearance, it requires very little[5] maintenance.

Don't let another minute go by without considering the difficulties that could be prevented[6] by putting up an Alabama link-chain fence. Cordially yours, (132)

Lesson 7, Page 31

27. Dear Mr. Brown: A number of leading citizens of our town feel that we should begin a trial promotion[1] campaign to attract more industry to this area. We are, therefore, attempting to organize a committee[2] to work on such a project. May we count on your help?

If our town is going to do something to protect the[3] future of our young people by bringing modern industry here, we need to organize an over-all plan and[4] advertise in the newspapers and other media. We can use your experience and ideas as an[5] advertising director to do everything possible to put this campaign across everywhere throughout the state.[6]

For the present, we only want to know that you will help us create a workable plan for the project. Before[7] the funds requested from the town council will be provided, everyone wants to know what our plans are.

If, for any[8] reason, your regular work might bias your action or create a problem, can you suggest someone else to whom we[9] could turn? Cordially yours, (186)

28. To the Staff: An envelope containing a quantity of samples of brown rayon was lost somewhere around the[1] building–possibly on the ground floor. If it is not found within the next few days, we probably will not be able[2] to meet one of the terms of a quotation: to match the color perfectly.

Every employee is urged to[3] check all papers and correspondence immediately. If you find the envelope, please call Julia Kane immediately.[4] Her extension is 613. John Barton (90)

29. Dear Miss Porter: In an effort to bring greater appreciation of modern poetry and music to the[1] public, your local radio station will soon produce a new program. We hope you will announce this new feature[2] to all the students in your school. May we ask in addition that you promote student interest further by providing[3] the background needed to enjoy fully the musical and poetry selections.

We will, of course, continue[4] our science series and will grant permission for high school students to take part in the program. There is one[5] provision, however. We never allow students in the studio without passes. These must be requested from[6] two to three weeks before the date selected. You may, however, obtain passes in whatever quantities you[7] need to make it possible for everybody to attend. Probably you should allow for an additional[8] one or two so that nobody will be turned away.

If you have any questions, or if there is anything[9] else that we can do to make this radio station a stronger link between the schools in this area and the[10] public, please do not hesitate to let us know. Cordially yours, (212)

30. Dear Miss Field: A number of years ago summer was thought of as the only proper time for taking a vacation.[1] That is no longer true. The winter months have become increasingly popular–in fact, January,[2] February, and March may soon rival June, July, and August.

Our agent has informed me that you requested information[3] about our low-cost flights to Europe, which we are presenting in the series called "Theater and the[4] Arts." You will notice in the enclosed pamphlet that there are two of these special trips–one features the theaters in London;[5] the other, the museums and the art galleries in Paris. This is an offer we are making only[6] between February 1 and March 26.

If you are interested in making such a trip, remember[7] that a small down payment will hold a reservation for you. Requests are coming in daily; so let us have your[8] remittance early if you don't want to be disappointed. Yours very truly, (174)

Lesson 8, Page 36

31. Dear Mrs. Washington: It is with exceedingly high hopes that we announce our furniture and furnishings show,[1] which will be held the last two weeks in March. We are not being immodest in saying that it will be the best in[2] Virginia.

We have arranged for specialists in home planning to come from Philadelphia and New York. Our guests will[3] be invited to confer with them on all furnishing problems.

Outstanding values in both domestic and[4] imported articles will be included in the displays. Committee members from the chamber of commerce previewed[5] the plans today and were most encouraging in their opinions.

We are reserving certain afternoons for club groups.[6] Needless to say, our objective in doing this is to give your members the opportunity to go through[7] the display rooms in comfort. We feel confident that you will approve this procedure, and we hope that your group can[8] soon decide upon a convenient day for attending the show.

Please write us promptly. After I hear from you, I will[9] be able to send you a letter of confirmation immediately. Very cordially yours, (198)

32. To Plant Managers in Houston, Los Angeles, and Portland: It is indeed embarrassing to report that a[1] competing firm has beaten us to the punch on our new eraser. Here at the home office, however, we are[2] not jumping to the conclusion that the situation is hopeless, as we shall have some features not covered by[3] the competition.

The product is as yet unfinished, but we have concluded that it would be disadvantageous[4] to get the eraser on the market immediately. To be impatient now might make it impossible[5] later to reach our particular goal.

We must insist, however, on a careful guarding of all information[6] related to this subject. All employees should be especially reminded of the confidential nature[7] of the new composition used for the eraser. No employee would knowingly give information, of course,[8] but each must be cautioned against thoughtless remarks in this connection. Remind your employees that it is to their[9] advantage to avoid any reference to this particular project.

Please send a strong memo on the subject[10] to everyone in your division. Emphasize the big investment that has gone into this project. C. G. Cummings[11] (221)

33. Dear Mr. Conrad: Would you like to increase your income? It would be advantageous to you in every way, we[1] are sure you will agree, and we can help you toward that goal.

Surveys show that the better educated man holds the[2] better job, and a better job means more income to do the things you and your family enjoy.

Perhaps you and[3] your family have not had a vacation for a long time; perhaps it is a more comfortable house that you[4] need; perhaps your problem is finding the needed income to send your children to college. Whatever your[5] situation, our extension course will help you to qualify for job advancement.

Send the enclosed card immediately[6] so that you can get started toward your goal. Yours truly, (130)

Lesson 9, Page 40

34. Dear Sarah: I just received an invitation to a luncheon from the director of public relations of[1] the Jender Cosmetic Company. I assume they are launching another new product and that the editors[2] of shopping columns for magazines and newspapers in this area are all invited.

No doubt your invitation[3] has already arrived. I'm hoping that you will be able to attend, for they do have well-arranged affairs;[4] but I shall delay sending in my reservation until I hear from you. Because you are just back from Europe[5] and probably have a backlog of desk work, I'm not sure you are going to accept.

Please be sure to let us[6] know as soon as you can whether I can count on your accompanying me. Sincerely, (136)

35. Dear Mrs. Mannerley: Of course you have fond recollections of a puppy that made many childhood days happy. May[1] we suggest you bring some of that joy to your children? We have several fine litters of collie pups. They are all of[2] a very gentle and intelligent strain. In fact, all of our Pleasant Valley Kennel dogs have given great[3] satisfaction to those who have purchased them.

Why don't you bring the children to our kennels and let them select the right[4] puppy. The puppies are priced at $150, and we know you will never have given your children[5] a more rewarding gift. They can lavish love on their pet, and the pet will return it. They will learn responsibility[6] in having to take care of their pet—feeding it, training and exercising it, brushing and bathing it.[7]

Why not stop in Sunday afternoon between two and six and spend a little while looking at the playful puppies[8] at our kennels? We know your children will immediately recognize the one puppy that just has to be theirs.[9] Driving directions for the kennels are enclosed. Cordially, (195)

36. Gentlemen: Yesterday I purchased a dining-room set and gave the clerk a definite delivery date of[1] July 1. I wonder if it would be possible to postpone delivery of this set until August 1.[2]

I had been told that the house that is being built for me would be ready for occupancy on or about June 20.[3] Just this morning I was informed that because of the very rainy weather the house cannot be completed for[4] several weeks more. The contractor assures me that I should be able to move in on or about July 10,[5] but there have been so many delays that I feel it would be advisable to postpone delivery of[6] the dining-room set until August 1.

I hope you will be able to arrange the change in delivery date[7] without too much inconvenience. I will be most appreciative. Cordially yours, (155)

37. To the Staff: It is particularly gratifying to report that yesterday we received word that Thomas[1] Regent, a director of our company, has been appointed to the governor's advisory staff.

This[2] recognition of Mr. Regent's excellent work in serving the public is also a great tribute to his[3] character.

Of course, it is unnecessary to remind anyone who knows him of the effort he has[4] expended to devise improvements in personnel policies in this company. These changes will prove worthwhile to[5] all those working in similar businesses. J. C. (110)

38. Dear Mr. Nativo: Thank you for your order for a new station wagon.

We are wondering whether you would[1] be satisfied with any other color than the one you chose. Several weeks ago an order was placed for[2] a similar model automobile, but the purchaser now finds that government business is going to take[3] him out of the country. He was not able, therefore, to take the car. His selection was a dark green, while yours was[4] light green.

If you would have no objection to this substitution, we could make immediate delivery;[5] otherwise we cannot give you a definite delivery date until the railroad strike is settled.

I hope[6] you will make an appointment to come in as soon as possible to see if you will be satisfied with the[7] substitution. We will hold the car for the remainder of this week but will have to have your positive acceptance[8] by a week from Saturday. Please let us know if you are interested in this suggestion. Yours truly, (178)

Lesson 10, Page 45

39. Gentlemen: As a result of a defect in the electric wiring recently installed in my home, I[1] have been without electricity for several days. Since you submitted an estimate on the job and then[2] a contract, you must admit that it is your responsibility to make the needed repairs as soon as[3] possible. I have already called you several times about this matter and also have written to you.

May I[4] hear from you by the end of the week, so that it will not be necessary for me to take further action. Very[5] truly yours, (102)

40. Dear John: I am pleased to report that almost all the arrangements for the political rally have been[1] completed. Did you know that more than one thousand tickets have been bought and paid for?

We have already had acknowledgments[2] from most of the politically important people in the county. In fact, it is altogether[3] possible that the governor himself will be present.

Everything seems to be shipshape as far as the program for[4] the day is concerned. We have several speakers lined up, and an agency is supplying music as well as[5] entertainers.

I also expect to be able shortly to submit a list of the food that will be needed.[6] A committee is working on the plans, but I do not have its report as yet. Peter (136)

41. Gentlemen: I was in your store this afternoon and placed a C. O. D. order for an electric iron. In[1] tonight's paper I discovered an advertisement stating that you are going to offer the same model for[2] practically half price the day after tomorrow—Thursday.

Naturally, I want to take advantage of the sale,[3] so please cancel the C. O. D. order. I will come in Thursday morning to purchase the iron myself and will[4] bring the order blank from the paper with me.

I am surprised and a little annoyed that the salesgirl did not tell[5] me about this sale. Is it possible she didn't know about it herself? Very truly yours, (116)

42. Dear Mr. Chipley: An article in this afternoon's newspaper pointed up the critical shortage of doctors[1] in this area. Certainly all of our citizens are aware of the situation here, and frankly I[2] am hopeful that the chamber of commerce will have suggestions to remedy the situation.

For one thing, I[3] believe an advertisement in medical papers and journals might bring success in attracting doctors to this area.[4] I am sure there are other ways, too, of doing so.

If everyone on the health committee of the chamber of[5] commerce will meet at my office at eleven o'clock on Friday, April 10, I feel sure we will be able[6] to start working toward our ultimate goal. I feel certain that you will all subscribe to any program that seems[7] practical and worthwhile.

Please telephone me as soon as you receive this note. I'm counting on your willingness to[8] attend this special meeting. Cordially yours, (167)

43. To the Staff: We are making long-range plans for our sales conference scheduled for the week of July 15. We'll meet[1] this year in the fifteenth-floor conference room.

I am enclosing the agenda covering the entire week. May[2] I call a few special items to your attention? Please note that we are starting at 8:30 Monday morning[3] instead of the usual 9 a.m. beginning time. The reason for this early start is to give Mr. Williams[4] a chance to greet you before he leaves to catch an early plane for Los Angeles. Also, please note that the Thursday[5] meetings will end at 9 p.m., so that we can get away early on Friday. Those are the only two time[6] changes from our usual schedule.

I liked the suggestions you sent in individually and in branch office[7] reports, and have incorporated most of them in the plans for the Wednesday afternoon sessions.

I think[8] everything else on the agenda speaks for itself. I'll see you early on the morning of July 15. Jerry[9] Franklin (181)

Lesson 11, Page 51

44. Dear Mr. Harrold: Your letter of January 31 requesting transfer of ownership of bonds, which[1] was postmarked February 1, did not reach us until February 6. Unfortunately, you forgot to[2] transmit the bonds with your request, and we wonder whether you have already discovered this oversight.

Perhaps[3] you would find it helpful to have our messenger pick up the bonds, after which we can take care of the transaction[4] and enter the new ownership very promptly.

If you will telephone, we shall be glad to make the arrangements.[5] We shall, of course, give the bonded messenger a letter of introduction. Very truly yours, (117)

45. Mr. Paragon: During the recent bad weather, we found that the typists and clerks could not gain entrance to their[1] working area because the security officer was delayed in reaching the building. Would it interfere[2] with your interpretation of internal security to see that keys are provided for at least one[3] of the supervisors on the office staff?

It would seem necessary to introduce some increase in security[4] personnel in order to include at least one responsible member of the office staff. I shall be[5] glad to arrange interviews with the staff and follow your specifications if you are inclined to support my[6] stand. J. C. Strong (123)

46. Dear Friend: Once again we are asking your support of our annual fund-raising campaign. The purpose of the drive[1] is familiar to you and your friends, but we would like to explain to our new neighbors that the

campaign has a twofold[2] purpose.

First and foremost, the major portion of the funds go toward perpetuating the annual Fourth of[3] July celebration, a "small town" tradition which unfortunately has become less and less a part of the[4] American scene. In addition, any surplus is invested in our Mutual Benefit Fund for[5] disabled firemen and for the families of deceased firemen.

Our program will follow the traditional[6] pattern. The day will begin with a parade, and will end with a superb fireworks display. In between, there will[7] be free rides and contests for the small fry, all carefully supervised; displays, exhibitions, and ball games for the[8] grownups; and other events of interest to both young and old. The local papers will be furnished with complete[9] details as they are worked out. Watch for them.

To prevent overcrowding and to assure the comfort, safety, and[10] convenience of you who are making the event possible, attendance will be limited to township residents[11] and their house guests only. The system that proved so successful in the past will be followed again this year. All adults[12] will have to show identification tags; children not accompanied by their parents will also be[13] required to display tags. The tags can be obtained from the uniformed fireman who will call at your home soon after[14] May 31. Or, if you wish, you may mail your contribution in the postpaid envelope. Be sure to include[15] your name and address and the number of tickets required. We will be glad to mail them to you. Very truly[16] yours, (321)

47. Dear Mr. Quincy: This will introduce to you Mr. George Addams, who has been in our employ for three years as[1] a junior bookkeeper. Mr. Addams finds it necessary to leave Chicago to seek employment in[2] Detroit.

Mr. Addams was a most successful employee in every way—he had an excellent relationship[3] with his supervisors as well as his co-workers. He did a superior job of bookkeeping and studied[4] at evening school so that he might advance. In fact, he was up for an advancement when he found it necessary[5] to leave us.

I do not hesitate to recommend George Addams to you for a position in your accounting[6] department. Cordially yours, (125)

Lesson 12, Page 56

48. Dear Mr. Marris: Congratulations on your recent appointment as Managing Editor of *Weekly News,*[1] published by the Gregory Publishing Company, Teaneck, New Jersey.

If you are like most of us, I know that,[2] while you are looking forward to the new assignment, you are dreading the inescapable chore that moving to[3] a new home involves. First of all, you have to find a competent moving company. Then you have to spend hours[4] packing and wrapping. And, of course, after you arrive at your new home, you have to spend more hours unwrapping and unpacking.[5]

Would you like to avoid all this? You can, you know. Just call the Joseph Harold Moving Company. We are prepared[6] to take care of all your moving problems.

When you have selected your moving date, let us know immediately.[7] Just before you get ready to leave, we will send our staff of efficient and competent packers to your home.[8] They will carefully wrap and pack all of your belongings. They will treat your cherished Haviland china with as much[9] care as you would. You have nothing to worry about. All pictures and mirrors will be individually crated[10] so that no harm can come to them. Of course, everything will be completely protected by insurance against[11] any loss or damage. Because of the competence of our staff, our claims are extremely small, so there is little[12] cause for alarm that any of your belongings will need to be replaced.

When moving day comes, our men will be there[13] at the hour you specify. They will load your belongings carefully and rapidly. You, Mrs. Marris, and[14] the children have nothing to worry about.

After arriving at your new home, the men will carefully and quickly[15] unload your belongings and place them exactly where you tell them to. If you like, our men will be happy to[16] lay the rugs and uncrate the pictures and mirrors. At your direction, they will place the clothing in the designated[17] closets.

Your moving can be accomplished effortlessly and pleasantly if you will call at the Joseph[18] Harold Moving Company, 2045 North Fourth Street. If you wish, you can telephone us at Chelsea 6-3198.[19] We will be glad to send a representative to discuss our very low rates with you and make the necessary[20] arrangements. He will also be happy to discuss any special packing or moving problems you may have. Yours[21] truly, (421)

49. Dear Mrs. Beach: You reserved a single room with bath for late arrival on Thursday, October 20, but[1] then you did not appear. Since you guaranteed payment for nonarrival, we are enclosing a bill for that night.[2]

In the future, if you cannot appear, we shall be glad to make no charge if you will give us twenty-four hours' notice[3] of cancellation. Very truly yours, (67)

50. Dear Fred: My niece, Mary Casey, is now bound for New York for the first time. She is looking forward to a brief[1] vacation before starting a job in Kansas City.

I hope you won't mind, but I did tell her that I would write[2] to see if you could arrange for tickets to two or three of the best shows. If there is a young man in your office[3] who would be willing to escort Mary, the treat is on me. She is an attractive girl with a charming personality.[4] I am enclosing a check to cover the cost of the tickets. Please let me know the amount of any[5] other expenses that may be necessary to insure an enjoyable visit for Mary—dinners,[6] taxi fares, etc.

It has been a long time since I have been to New York, but you'll find me dropping in[7] on you one of these days on my way to Washington.

Thanks for anything you do to see that Mary has an[8] unforgettable vacation.

Best wishes to you and Jessie. Sincerely yours, (174)

51. Dear Mr. Jeffrey: You are cordially invited to attend the faculty dinner that we are planning for[1] Friday, June 16, honoring our own Dr. Gerald Gray, who has just returned from an extensive lecture tour[2] of the Far East.

Immediately after the banquet on Friday, Dr. Gray will present one of his stimulating[3] lectures. You are familiar with his reputation, I know. Dr. Gray is planning to illustrate his[4] presentation with some excellent colored slides that he made while visiting these interesting places.

Reservations[5] must reach our office no later than Friday, May 26. To be sure that there is a place for you, Mr.[6] Jeffrey, why not sign and return the enclosed reservation card at once. If you prefer to telephone or to[7] send a telegram to make your reservation certain, please do so.

You won't want to miss this exciting event.[8] Sincerely yours, (163)

52. Dear Miss Wolf: You are right; we are wrong. We have rechecked our records, as you suggested, and we find that you had made[1] your regular monthly payment. Unfortunately, errors such as these occasionally occur; and we are[2] genuinely sorry that we have caused you some embarrassment.

Won't you please set our minds at ease by visiting[3] Vollmer's Department Store soon. You are one of our best customers, and we want to be sure that you continue to[4] be our friend.

Continuing the policy that we established several years ago, Vollmer's Department Store will[5] be closed on Saturdays during July and August. We shall again be open on Saturdays beginning[6] September.

All of us here hope that you and your family have a very pleasant and safe summer. Very truly[7] yours, (141)

Lesson 13, Page 63

53. Dear Mr. Johnston: Circumstances will not permit my undertaking a sales trip to Stamford for another[1] month or two, and I am too selfish to want anyone else to make the trip! If your department managers' meeting[2] can be postponed just a few weeks, I would be more than delighted to participate in your program.

Next week I[3] will be visiting our plants in Harrisburg and Pittsburgh; then I go to Johnstown, Lexington, Nashville, Birmingham,[4] and Jacksonville. I expect to return to the office in about two weeks.

I probably shall use the following[5] two weeks to clear up most of the accumulation of desk work. However, I could be with you the week of[6] May 10—just five weeks from now. I had planned to visit Evanston and Springfield, Illinois, and Davenport, Iowa,[7] first, but I could stop in each of those cities on my way back from California and Washington. I know I[8] sound like an advertisement for an airline with such jumping around, but you will understand that it cannot be[9] avoided.

Let me know how I can best fit into your program. Which would be the better time—the week of May 10[10] or May 17? It is understood that you have first choice. Very truly yours, (214)

54. Gentlemen: We should like to resume our telephone service as of May 15 at 24 Shady Drive, Greenfield.[1]

When we had you disconnect our telephone, we expected to be in Yorktown until June 1. We shall, however,[2] be returning two weeks sooner, and we assume you can arrange to have our telephone ready for use on[3] our arrival. Yours very truly, (67)

55. Dear Mr. Hart: Every self-made man knows that work—and good, hard work—was partly responsible for his getting where[1] he is today. He also knows that even though he may have started working in his teens, he had to keep up with[2] the trends and changing events to continue to go up that ladder.

Even presidents of large corporations[3] are going to school. Many are attending seminars given in company conference rooms under the[4] direction of outside management specialists; others attend many meetings in hotels and convention halls; still[5] others are returning to their colleges or universities for a study of humanities.

Regardless[6] of where you are in your company, the chances of your going somewhere "to school" this next year are four to one.[7] With that thought in mind, we would like to have you meet Mr. Jack Welch, our management consultant, who is well acquainted[8] with educational opportunities available.

Mr. Welch has just completed a tour of twenty[9] cities in the United States, from Seattle, Washington, to Birmingham, Alabama. On his way to[10] Pittsburgh, he will make a slight detour and stop in Cleveland and Detroit. While he is in Pittsburgh, we will act as his[11] agent. We have, therefore, arranged a luncheon for him, and we are inviting fifty of the leading businessmen[12] of our city to be guests at that luncheon. We shall be meeting at the Oxford Hotel at twelve noon on Friday,[13] May 12. We hope that your schedule will permit you to be our guest that day, Mr. Hart, and that you will be able[14] to stay for a little while to chat with Mr. Welch. Just mail the enclosed card letting us know your decision.[15] Cordially yours, (302)

56. Dear Customer: Just a single, moderate-sized order from the exciting bargain circulars enclosed can save[1] you $10 or more! That's how much lower these prices are than those in most retail stores.

Also, you needn't send us one[2] penny of the amount until you see and try our merchandise and prove how much you save! What is more, anything[3] can be returned and there'll be no charge.

You don't find $10 or more this easily every day. Why not put[4] your free trial order forms in the mail to us today? Yours for savings, (93)

Lesson 14, Page 67

57. Mr. Guest: Last week our president, Mr. Lake, advocated a change in our company's insurance program.[1] Before inaugurating the new program, however, he would like to investigate all the types of insurance[2] available to make sure that we get the very best.

You have an excellent insurance background; consequently,[3] Mr. Lake has asked that the job of studying various insurance programs be delegated to[4] you. As you know, we have had several studies made during the past two years; to avoid duplication of[5] information, you may want to look at the figures that have already been gathered. I will see if I can locate[6] some of this material here and send it to you today.

Could you give this matter your attention during the[7] next month? It seems to me that your best contribution can be made by checking into what is available to[8] see which plan is most adequate for our requirements and the cost of instituting the plan.

Mr. Lake has[9] asked me to express his gratitude for your help. After you are through with your study, he will no doubt thank you in[10] person. By the way, how do you like your new location? Jerry Case (213)

58. Dear Mrs. Nestor: I am sorry that I cannot excuse your son Jimmy on the basis of the explanation[1] offered for his absence from classes last Tuesday. It is, I will agree, unusual for us to refuse[2] to accept an excuse offered by a parent.

There were a number of absences on the day in question, and[3] an inquiry at the local theater indicates that your son, along with several other boys, spent the[4] day there.

Surely, therefore, he could not have been suffering from tonsillitis, as the excuse indicates.

I am[5] sure you are eager for Jimmy to have every advantage that an education offers. You should know,[6] however, that his frequent absences are responsible for his failure to meet the requirements of several[7] courses.

Aptitude tests indicate that Jimmy could be an outstanding student, but his frequent absences[8] and his attitude are preventing him from making satisfactory grades, despite this aptitude.

I hope you[9] will co-operate by making certain that any subsequent absences on Jimmy's part are accompanied[10] by valid excuses. Very truly yours, (207)

59. Dear Doctor Fisher: I must apologize for the delay in sending you a check for the neuritis treatments[1] that I received last month. I returned today from a trip to Atlantic City and other parts of the state and[2] found your reminder waiting for me.

I am feeling quite well now. Before I received the treatments the pains almost[3] drove me frantic; lately, however, I have had no pain whatsoever. I attribute this improvement to the[4] excellent way in which you handled my case. Cordially yours, (91)

60. Dear Mr. Collins: Your contribution at the meeting last Monday night is very much appreciated.[1] Frankly, I don't know what we would have done without your help, since our speaker was, of course, snowbound and it was too late to[2] obtain another on such short notice.

Your willingness to organize a panel in a few hours is all[3] that made it possible to hold the meeting. Thanks once more for all that you and the members of your panel did to[4] make the evening a success. Sincerely, (87)

61. Dear Mrs. Gardiner: Everyone at Johnston's joins with me in extending to you an invitation to participate[1] in the formal dedication ceremonies for our new building at 220 East Market Street in[2] Springfield.

The ceremonies will be at 4:30 p.m., Tuesday, March 7, and will be followed by a[3] reception and dinner at 6 p.m. at the Dodds Hotel.

If you are able to come, please fill in the enclosed card[4] and return it to me so that we may make our plans. Most sincerely, (93)

Lesson 15, Page 72

62. Dear Mrs. Held: Your mailman will soon bring you a recent issue of *World Travel.* We hope that through this magazine[1] you will enjoy a tour of the English countryside and visits to the historic castles of England. In[2] addition to the "tour," there is a capsule history of Great Britain and a full-color feature on its royal[3] family. Future issues will cover Canada, Germany, Puerto Rico, and the U.S.A., to mention[4] just a few of the interesting places you can visit right at home.

We should like to have you take advantage[5] of a significant saving by accepting the anniversary subscription rates offered on the convenient[6] order form enclosed. Cordially yours, (128)

63. Dear Carol: As you know, ever since Hawaii became our fiftieth state, our Business Girls Club has been trying[1] to get enough members to sign up so that we could take advantage of a special two-week trip planned especially for us.[2]

At this writing, we have 47 who have made reservations and we need only 3 more. Wouldn't you[3] like to be one of those 3 who will join us and make that total 50? From the picture folders we have sent you[4] before of this beautiful paradise of the Pacific, you know that we shall have the most up-to-date[5] accommodations at the three hotels we shall stop at—in Honolulu, Hilo, and Kona.

There are only two weeks left[6] before our final deadline. Do let me hear from you before then. Sincerely yours, (134)

64. Are You Efficient or Do You Just Get By?

Here is a report of a survey of office executives made by *Today's Secretary.*

Filing Feud.[1] Executives, practically to a man, said that they do not want filing to accumulate. They are aware that[2] filing is not a joy unsurpassed, but they feel that it should be done daily. If filing is put off, there are long[3] delays when they need a certain letter for quick reference; and there is embarrassment when a letter is[4] requested by another member of the organization and cannot be located immediately.[5]

Telephone Trouble. If it is really necessary to call Mary or Jim once in a blue moon and if you[6] keep the conversation to a minimum, executives say, "O.K." Urgent personal business they understand;[7] but they wholeheartedly object to long, unnecessary, frequent personal telephone calls during office[8] hours.

Other telephone laments were these: failure of a secretary to recognize voices of frequent[9] callers; being slack in reporting telephone messages; not getting the name of a caller, or getting it[10] incorrectly; forgetting to try a number again after the line has been busy; and answering the telephone[11] by merely saying "hello" instead of stating the proper department or company name.

Desk Desertion.[12] Executives realize that you and your posture chair aren't attached for keeps, but they do wish that you wouldn't leave[13] it alone so much. Businessmen ask that you let your conscience be your guide and that you be at your desk when you know[14] you will be needed. There are times when routine office duties make it necessary for you to be away from[15] your desk. They request that at these times you let them know where you will be—or at least ask someone to answer your[16] telephone until you return. (326)

Lesson 16, Page 77

65. Dear Mrs. Strong: We are happy to send you, as a gift certificate holder, the enclosed schedule of[1] performances of the plays to be presented by the Theater Academy during its summer season. We are[2] delighted to announce that, in addition to Shakespeare, we shall give some of Victor Herbert's operettas.

It is[3] your special privilege to be in the first group to select dates. We are holding the best seat locations until[4] April 1 for you. Kindly circle the dates of your choice, selecting one performance of each of the six plays, and[5] return the form to the Theater Academy in the enclosed envelope.

During April and May, we shall be[6] presenting a revival of *The Winter's Tale* for our annual school program. We are offering you an[7] opportunity to see this play on selected evenings at a discount of $2 a seat: Friday nights,[8] a $5.50 seat for $3.50; Saturday nights, a $6 seat for $4.[9] If you wish to take advantage of this offer, please indicate the date and the number of seats you want on the[10] form and enclose your check for the total amount. Very truly yours, (213)

66. Dear Mr. Yale: For a great number of people the question is not how much capital do I have but how much[1] income do I have.

Most of us do not want to "dip" into the capital we have. It is a bad financial[2] practice because spent capital is not easily replenished and because, once spent, it can no longer provide[3] income.

Those who look ahead to their financial future must solve two important problems:

1. How much are they able[4] or willing to set aside out of their salaries?

2. How shall they invest this money so that it will do[5] them the most good?

The first problem is a personal one and can be solved only by the individual[6] himself. There is no formula. Personal inclinations of the family involved are the prime factor, of course.[7]

But the question of how to put the money to work does lend itself to certain common-sense rules. If you will check[8] the enclosed card, Mr. Yale, we shall be glad to submit a plan to you through the mail. You'll not be annoyed by[9] anyone ringing your doorbell. You owe it to yourself and family to get this information. Cordially yours, (199)

67. Miss Pindery: Would any of the employees in your division be interested in overtime work for[1] approximately a three-month period? We are looking for additional help in the billing department[2] for the months of November through January.

Those interested should be told that they will be expected to[3] report for work Monday and Thursday evenings from six to eight. They will be paid $2.75 an[4] hour on this job.

Please be sure to let me know about those people on your staff whom you would recommend and who[5] might be interested in this opportunity for extra income. I hope you will be able to forward[6] the names of two or three prospects to me soon. J. G. Devlin (131)

68. Dear Mr. Judd: The Board of Directors has approved your recommendation to extend an invitation to[1] buyers and assistant buyers to attend a special showing of the new materials that will be used in[2] our dress and suit line this fall.

They have requested that you prepare an announcement that will stir up general interest[3] in the event and an outline of the campaign you have in mind for promoting the fall line, including[4] letters you will write and the program to be sent out in advance of the showing.

Before you proceed on your own with[5] further plans, please come to my office and let's discuss the details outlined above. We will not submit any[6] further plans until we can be quite certain they will be received and approved without question and that we will be[7] given the signal to proceed. Fred Kerr (147)

Lesson 17, Page 82

69. Dear Mr. Johnson: I wish I could have an opportunity to tell your management team why you should look into[1] the opportunities afforded by group membership in our life insurance program. Although the plan is[2] not offered to the general public, it is under Federal jurisdiction.

Won't you look over the plan[3] outlined in the enclosed booklet, and then discuss the rates with some of your top men? If you would like to have additional[4] copies of the booklet, please give me the name of the person to whom they should be addressed and the number[5] I should supply.

Other firms in this area who are participating in our plan are listed in the booklet.[6] I am sure any of them would be glad to tell you about the successful introduction of this program in[7] their companies. Past experience proves that employees appreciate the increased benefits that membership[8] in our plan offers them.

Employee payments, of course, are by means of monthly payroll deductions. Payment to us[9] would follow your receipt of an invoice for the total premium.

Please use the enclosed reply card or telephone[10] me so that I may explain the special benefits your employees will receive through the protection our plan[11] provides. Cordially yours, (224)

70. Dear Miss Carter: This year's card party to raise scholarship loan funds was a marked success.

A committee is going[1] to meet on May 15 to make the decision as to those who will be granted loans from the proceeds and the amount[2] of each loan.

If you have any students who wish to apply, and who qualify under the regulations[3] outlined in the printed form attached, please have them complete the necessary application and submit it to[4] the chairman of the loan committee right away. Cordially yours, (92)

71. Mr. Forman: Several items of our office equipment need to be replaced as soon as possible.

Two[1] of our adding machines are not functioning properly. In fact, if we are awarded the contract for auditing[2] the King Oil Company's stations, we will be severely handicapped unless these machines are replaced.[3]

Several typewriters should also be replaced. Three of them are of rather ancient vintage. I would like to replace them[4] with electric machines to improve the appearance of our correspondence and reports and, at the same time,[5] reduce fatigue of our typists and thereby increase production. I would recommend that we consider converting[6] to electric typewriters as additional replacements are required, with perhaps one or two manuals[7] reserved for emergency use.

I am attaching a report on several adding machines left with us[8] for demonstration and trial. The people who will be using this equipment have had an oportunity[9] to use each machine and are generally agreed that electric Banner best meets our needs. May I have your[10] authorization to order two?

I am also attaching a report on the furniture and equipment on[11] hand to date showing the make and model of all office machines, the dates purchased, and the amount paid. I have also[12] indicated when, in my opinion, each item may need to be replaced. John Day (255)

72. The Competent Secretary Saves the Employer's Time

Let us examine the procedures of at least three competent secretaries.

One saves time for her employer[1] by writing letters "on approval" that come in for her employer to answer. She gathers the facts pertaining[2] to the question at hand and then drafts a reply just as she believes her employer would write it. Many of the[3] letters are "tricky," but very often the employer does not have to make a single change.

This same secretary[4] saves time for her employer, too, by knowing when to ask questions. It is no disgrace to ask questions, although some[5] young stenographers and secretaries seem to think so. This secretary knows when she knows, but she also knows[6] when she *doesn't* know and then she will ask.

Another secretary saves time for her employer by her tactful[7] handling of dozens of people who visit the office each day. Her employer said, "My secretary is[8] able to talk with people with tact and courtesy and turn over to me only those who need my special[9] attention."

Our third employer was singing the praises of his secretary by saying, "She always puts work on[10] my desk that I can sign without correction. She knows that every time something has to be given back to her,[11] it is a waste of my time as well as hers."

The secretary who has good technical skills, can compose letters[12] as her employer would compose them, and who greets callers in such a way that they will not feel slighted if the "boss"[13] does not see them is indeed worth a great deal to any employer. (273)

Lesson 18, Page 87

73. Dear Member: Our regular monthly meeting—the last until September—is scheduled for Thursday night, June 14.[1] At that time Mr. S. C. Long, director of the Pittsfield Hospital, will give a brief lecture on[2] hospital record keeping and accounting as practiced in his institution. We believe this presentation will[3] be extremely beneficial to all of us. Also, we have scheduled an excellent film entitled[4] "Efficient Hospital Operation," which will be especially helpful to those who have recently entered the field.[5]

Please refer to the official program for complete details. We hope you will be with us.[6] Sincerely, (122)

74. Dear Miss Strong: You will be pleased to know that after considerable checking, benefits were approved for your[1] hospital care. There would have been no delay in investigating your eligibility for coverage if you[2] had given the most recent identification card to the hospital.

Please dispose of all hospital[3] identification cards which you may have in your possession that are no longer current. In the future, be[4] sure to use only the identification card bearing the contract number shown above to insure prompt[5] settlement of any claim. If you don't have a card bearing the above number and you are enrolled through a group, you[6] may request a new card by contacting the group under which you are currently enrolled.

If you have paid the bills,[7] the proper adjustment in your account will come directly from the hospital. We are glad to have been of[8] assistance. Cordially, Admission Processing Department (170)

75. Dear Mr. Carter: Welcome to the growing list of satisfied customers who say, "Charge it, please" at the Nashville[1] Department Store. Your account is ready for use when you next visit our store. Our entire staff stands ready to[2] do everything possible to make your shopping here pleasant and satisfying.

You will receive a monthly[3] statement of purchases made shortly after our closing date for billings, the 20th of each month. Then you may[4] have until the 15th of the next month to pay your account. From the fine way that you have handled charge accounts at[5] other stores, we know that you will make prompt payments.

We invite you to enjoy the convenience of your charge account[6] to the fullest by taking advantage of the many special services offered by our store, such as telephone[7] shopping, free parking in the lot at the back of the store, prompt and efficient delivery throughout the city[8] and suburbs, and gift wrapping.

Come in often to shop or just to browse. You are always welcome at the Nashville[9] Department Store. Sincerely yours, (186)

76. Dear Mr. Adams: You may not know it, but the chances are 15 to 1 that you're working extremely hard. By[1] "working extremely hard," I mean working under too great pressure with needless effort for the net results that you[2] attain.

How can I make that statement? Because for over seventy-five years my company has studied the work[3] methods of thousands of business and professional people like you. We've been able to show 14 out of 15[4] of them a pleasant short cut to accomplishment.

You are probably as busy as we are and may not have time[5] now to examine the many advantages of Smith's latest worksaver. Assuming that is so, we have prepared[6] a 12-page free booklet called *Making More Time.* It is an idea-packed, step-by-step analysis of modern[7] executive work methods. It shows how busy men can keep work from piling up and get more done with much less effort. It[8] is an eye-opening book, full of helpful ideas for simplifying your job.

I am eager to see that you[9] get a copy. All you have to do is to initial and return this letter in the enclosed envelope.[10] Cordially, (202)

77. Gentlemen: Did our national advertising campaign result in another spurt in orders for you? We are[1] now ready to introduce a local promotion program that has set a great record wherever it has been[2] used.

It is important that you keep careful records of all sales of this merchandise over the period of[3] these efforts. We shall need this information to determine the effectiveness of these two types of sales promotion[4] and to work out any changes and improvements that would result in even better sales next year.

We are confident[5] you will find that sales of our products will be better than ever. Very truly yours, (115)

Lesson 19, Page 92

78. How to Get a Promotion

Is there a magic formula for getting a raise or promotion? Can it be put into words? A group of[1] career men and women attending a meeting heard one statement recently that may be a formula. The speaker[2] was Thomas C. Boushall, president of The Bank of Virginia. He put it this way: "Only those will be[3] rapidly advanced in business and professional life who understand that they must render service greater than[4] that for which they are immediately paid."

The careerists agreed. Then they began to apply that yardstick to[5] the business people they knew. They ticked off on their fingers the secretaries and junior executives they could[6] honestly say were "giving a little extra steam."

Most of them didn't get beyond the third or fourth finger.

Most[7] of the careerists felt their list was short because so many young people will give that little "extra steam" only[8] after they have been recognized and not before. It doesn't work that way, however. They must *first* "render service[9] greater than that for which they are immediately paid." (190)

79. Dear Mabel: You asked for some advice in helping you to get and keep a good job. First of all, I think you should[1] know that an employer will hire you for three main reasons: (1) the kind of person you are, (2) what you can[2] do, (3) your willingness and ability to grow.

The kind of person you are includes everything—from how you[3] look, how you act, and how you speak to how you think. Yes, even how you *think*, because thinking influences your actions[4] on the job. If you look upon what you do as just another job, it will show in your work; but, if you look[5] upon it as an opportunity, that, too, will show in what you do. What you can do includes your skills —your[6] ability to turn out a good letter in a reasonable length of time. I don't think I need say anything[7] more about that now. Most stenographers could shorten their transcribing time too.

Your willingness and ability[8] to grow are of the utmost importance. I think I can best illustrate this briefly by the following story.[9] A young secretary in a publishing company was taking dictation from her employer. The employer[10] used an author's name, and the secretary said, "How do you spell that name?"

The employer answered, "Why, you have the book[11] right on your desk." The secretary answered, "Oh, I didn't even know it."

In other words, this secretary[12] wasn't interested in becoming acquainted with the company's product—the books. Chances are that she wasted[13] spare moments. Certainly, she wasn't growing.

Mabel, I could go on and on. This is enough for you to think[14] about right now. Sincerely yours, (286)

80. Dear Mr. Cunningham: The technical training in which you are interested is being offered in about[1] three weeks. We have had to postpone the class because several members of our faculty have been ill—our failure[2] to write you about the opening of the class wasn't an oversight.

Just as soon as the final date is settled,[3] we will give you further details as to the place of meeting and the exact time. This you can be certain of[4] right now: you will like the program offerings and will be pleased with our excellent instructors.

You'll be hearing from[5] us again soon. Cordially yours, (106)

81. Dear Mr. Ballard: Is your Students Organization looking for ways to make money? We have a fine line of[1] products that

should find ready customers at most of your school games and social functions. They appeal to college[2] as well as high school students.

Samples of several items that we think will sell most readily are being shipped[3] to you today. As soon as you are ready to place a purchase order, fill in the special form enclosed. We will[4] be pleased to bill you on open account.

From time to time we prepare display cards to promote the sale of new book[5] and record titles. If you can use material of this type, be sure to advise us in the appropriate[6] section of the order blank. Cordially yours, (128)

82. Dear Mr. Murdock: One of the direct benefits of membership in the Office Managers Guild is your[1] subscription to our monthly bulletin. In the next issue, for instance, we are having a report on government[2] salaries for clerical employees. You will find much valuable and factual information that will[3] be useful as a basis for revising your own salary standards. Another article which will perhaps[4] be of even more pertinent interest: How to Ask For and Get Co-operation That Will Increase Production.[5]

As chairman of the Membership Committee, I am extending an invitation to you to join our[6] association. You will find membership in the Guild will make for an easier way of life in taking over the[7] responsibilities of your new position.

Why not reply immediately by sending in the application[8] form completed. Then plan to join us for our monthly luncheon in the Convention Room of the Market Street Hotel[9] the first Monday of next month. Cordially, (187)

83. Dear Mrs. Cummings: We are likely to be suffering a critical shortage of fuel oil during the present[1] strike. Since our Mayor has asked all of us to ration our consumption of fuel during this crisis, we would like to[2] recommend to you our small electric heater described in the enclosed literature.

Portable electric[3] heaters have been used in your neighborhood for some time; however, none has been on the market until now like the[4] one described. To see this heater, just stop in at our store at 27 Wilmington Boulevard, or our[5] agent will gladly deliver one to your home and demonstrate its outstanding features. Cordially yours, (118)

Lesson 20, Page 98

84. Secretarial Attributes

A business executive was telling a group of secretarial students, soon to be graduated, about[1] the best secretary he ever had.

"She understood the importance of public relations—and good public[2] relations means creating and keeping good will not only with your customers but with your fellow workers. She[3] created this good will in many different ways. Because she had cultivated a good memory, she[4] could remember all our regular customers and it made them feel important to be greeted by name when they[5] telephoned me or walked into my office.

"She took care of my appointment book and checked up on me in a tactful[6] way if my work fell behind schedule. If I was tied up in a conference, she knew when I should be[7] interrupted and when not. She used good judgment and she wasn't afraid to take a chance. Neither did she think it beneath[8] her to sharpen my pencils and fill my pens. She also did that occasional personal errand as a part[9] of her job."

A good secretary does not just happen. She is well trained. A beginner does not often start as[10] a secretary. If she has good training in school or college and has confidence in herself and her ability,[11] she should be willing to start as a stenographer until she "knows the ropes" and has her feet on the ground. Then[12] after she has acquired this experience and a certain amount of polish and poise, she will be ready[13] to fill that much-envied post of secretary. (269)

85. Dear Neighbor: You are no doubt aware of the strong and persistent efforts to place a giant jetport, the largest[1] in the world, in your neighborhood. Our permanent local committee, named on this letterhead, has been formed to[2] express opposition to this threatening proposal.

Should this proposal ever become a reality,[3] we earnestly believe that it would bring about chaos in housing, schools, taxes, and highway congestion. Our pleasant[4] suburban way of life would be gone. We would never again be the fine residential town we now are.

Surely[5] you feel as we do and will send a contribution in the enclosed envelope to help us continue our efforts[6] to combat the proposed jetport.

Funds must be available to provide for legal, public relations, and[7] technical services, as well as office expenses, to carry on an effective program of opposition.[8] We are, therefore, appealing for contributions from the residents of our town as well as from those in surrounding[9] towns.

Our committee meets the first Monday of the month at 8 p.m. in the Civic Center. Please feel free to[10] attend our meetings and keep informed on the progress we are making. Very sincerely, (216)

86. Dear Mrs. Bennett: We are concerned about the fact that your charge account has not been used recently. If there has[1] been a change in your name or address or if we have been at fault in any way, please let us know.

We are very[2] anxious to keep your account on our books, so that when you come in to shop, it will be a convenience to you. We[3] certainly don't like to lose old friends, as they are responsible for the growth and success of our business.[4] (Incidentally, we opened our first store just 135 years ago.)

This spring our seven stores, listed at the[5] top of this letter, have their usual complete assortments of smart, quality fashions, accessories, and gifts[6] for every member of the family at our usual low prices. We are opening our eighth store this[7] fall.

Easter time is the time to shop, and your charge account ought to be particularly useful. Of course, as a[8] charge customer, you receive advance information about fashions as well as special sales.

Every member[9] of our organization looks forward to serving you. We will be most grateful to you if you will return the[10] enclosed card and continue your friendly interest in our stores. Very truly yours, (214)

87. Dear Alumnus: A 53 per cent increase in contributions in three years! That is the story of the recent[1] Alumni Fund success at your university.

More and more graduates are donating to the[2] university, as its fame and achievements continue to grow.

In the thirtieth annual campaign which closed June 30,[3] I am proud to report that the Alumni Fund drive broke all records. A total of $403,416[4] was given by 19,850 graduates.

There is an opportunity for even[5] greater accomplishment in the thirty-first Alumni Fund campaign now underway. We are attempting an[6] exciting project this year. Alumni may specifically contribute to the library and browsing lounge in the[7] new student center. The magnificent building is scheduled to be completed next fall.

Thus your contribution,[8] if you wish, will be earmarked for the library and browsing lounge. You may, of course, give for unrestricted purposes,[9] as in the past, if you prefer. The enclosed form gives you the choice of how your contribution is to be used.

You[10] may make your gift to the thirty-first Alumni Fund campaign now—or pledge a contribution to be made later.[11] Either way, I hope you will fill in the form and return it to the alumni office at your earliest[12] convenience. Sincerely yours, (244)